Warm & Fuzzy Crochet

EDITED BY BOBBIE MATELA

the Needlecraft® Shop

EDITOR Bobbie Matela
ART DIRECTOR Brad Snow
PUBLISHING SERVICES DIRECTOR Brenda Gallmeyer

ASSOCIATE EDITORS Kathy Wesley,
Mary Ann Frits
ASSISTANT ART DIRECTOR Nick Pierce
COPY SUPERVISOR Michelle Beck
COPY EDITORS Nicki Lehman,
Mary O'Donnell
TECHNICAL EDITOR Tammy Hebert
TECHNICAL ARTIST Nicole Gage

GRAPHIC ARTS SUPERVISOR Ronda Bechinski
BOOK DESIGN Brad Snow
GRAPHIC ARTISTS Glenda Chamberlain,
Edith Teegarden
PRODUCTION ASSISTANT June Sprunger

PHOTOGRAPHY Tammy Christian,
Don Clark, Matthew Owen,
Jackie Schaffel
PHOTO STYLISTS Tammy Nussbaum,
Tammy M. Smith

CHIEF EXECUTIVE OFFICER John Robinson
PUBLISHING DIRECTOR David J. McKee
MARKETING DIRECTOR Dan Fink

Copyright © 2006 The Needlecraft Shop
Berne, Indiana 46711

FIRST PRINTING 2006
LIBRARY OF CONGRESS CONTROL NUMBER 2005938067
HARDCOVER ISBN 1-57367-231-9
SOFTCOVER ISBN 1-57367-232-7
Printed in China

Every effort has been made to ensure the accuracy and completeness of
the instructions in this book. However, we cannot be responsible for human
error or for the results when using materials other than those specified in the
instructions, or for variations in individual work.

Introduction

Get ready for some *Warm & Fuzzy Crochet!* This collection offers projects that combine soft textural yarns with an array of designs to inspire you.

Our Cozy Delights include fashion accessories, like hats, scarves and leg warmers.

The Sensuous Wraps are just the thing for warming shoulders and are perfectly wonderful gift ideas.

There is a scrumptious selection of fashion sweaters, vests, shrugs and jackets included with our Wearable Warmers.

Every bed and sofa needs to have an afghan to keep our footsies warm. So our Snuggle-Up Afghans designs are destined to be crocheted for their practicality, but appreciated for how they add textural color accents to our rooms.

Since babies are so much fun to crochet for, you'll find sweaters, booties, hats and afghans in our selection for Huggable Little Ones.

As you can tell, we are really excited about this collection of designs and hope that you will enjoy creating warm feelings with your crochet hook!

With warm & fuzzy thoughts,

Bobbie Matela

Contents

Cozy Delights

Cozy crocheted accessories like hats,
scarves, leg warmers and a muff are
great for warming up your wardrobe.

Make It Furry Hat & Muff

DESIGN BY MARIA MERLINO

SKILL LEVEL

FINISHED SIZE
Hat: One size fits most
Muff: 10 x 8 inches, excluding strap

MATERIALS
 TLC Heathers medium (worsted) weight yarn:
5 oz/260 yds/141g #2470 teal *(A)*
 Moda Dea Fur Ever bulky (chunky) weight
eyelash yarn:
7 oz/195 yds/196g #3529 aqua marine *(B)*
Size M/13/9mm crochet hook or size needed to
obtain gauge
Tapestry needle
7 decorative vintage buttons (optional)

GAUGE
3 sts = 2 inches; 4 rows = 2 inches

PATTERN NOTES
Join with slip stitch unless otherwise stated.

Muff is worked in rounds on wrong side; mark
beginning of rounds.

Instructions

MUFF
Rnd 1: With 2 strands of A, ch 24, join to form a
ring. Ch 1, sc in same sp and in each rem ch.

Rnd 2: Attach B (3 strands total), [sc in next st,
2 sc in next] around. *(36 sts)*

Rnds 3–19: Sc in each st. At end of rnd 19, drop B.

Rnd 20: Sc in each st.

STRAP
Note: *Strap is worked in rows.*

Row 1: Sc in next 2 sts, turn.

Row 2: Ch 1, pick up B, sc in each st, turn.

Row 3: Ch 1, sc in each st, turn.

Rep row 3 until strap measures 34 inches or desired
length. Fasten off leaving a long end for sewing.

With tapestry needle, sew strap to opposite side.

HAT

Note: *For **dec,** [yo, pull up lp in next st] twice, yo and draw through all 3 lps on hook.*

Rnd 1: With 2 strands of A and 1 strand of B held tog, ch 14, dc in 3rd ch from hook, and in next 11 chs, working along opposite side in unused lps of beg ch, dc in next 12 chs, join with sl st in first dc. *(24 sts)*

Rnd 2: Ch 3 *(counts as a dc now and throughout)*, 2 dc in next st, [dc in next st, 2 dc in next st] around, join. *(36 sts)*

Rnds 3–7: Ch 3, dc in each st around, join.

Rnd 8: Ch 3, dc in next 3 sts, **dec** *(see Note)* in next 2 sts, [dc in next 4 sts, dec in next 2 sts] around, join. *(30 sts)*

Rnd 9: Drop B, sc in each st around.

Fasten off and weave in all ends.

OPTIONAL BUTTON TRIM
Separate a yd of A into 2 plys. Use this for sewing. Sew 3 buttons in a triangular shape in the center front of muff. Sew 4 buttons on a diagonal on side of hat. 🍓

Fun Hairpin Lace Set

DESIGN BY ZELDA WORKMAN

SKILL LEVEL
INTERMEDIATE

FINISHED SIZE
Tam: One size fits most adults.
Scarf: Approximately 100 inches long x 5½ inches wide.

MATERIALS
5 BULKY Lion Suede bulky (chunky) weight yarn:
12 oz/488 yds/340g #133 spice
Size J/10/6mm crochet hook or size needed to obtain gauge
Adjustable hairpin loom or one that is 2½ inches wide
Tapestry needle

GAUGE
Exact gauge not necessary for these projects.

Instructions

BASIC HAIRPIN STRIP
Step 1: To beg, make a slip knot on hook; wrap yarn from behind loom around right prong to front of loom. In front of loom, position hook with slip knot in center; hook yarn and pull through slip knot.

Step 2: Hold hook upright and turn loom to left (pulling right side toward you and around) so that yarn wraps around 2nd prong, which is on the right after loom is turned. Inserting hook upward between strands, sc around front strand of lp on left prong. *(1 st complete)*

Rep step 2 twice to complete next st.

SCARF
STRIPS
Set adjustable loom at 2½-inches wide. Following instructions for Basic Hairpin Strip, make 4 strips each 220 sts long.

JOINING STRIPS
Lay strips next to each other on a flat surface, keeping center sts straight and not twisting the strips. To join first 2 strips, beg with right-hand strip and insert hook through bottom left lp of first strip; hook right bottom lp of left strip and pull through lp on hook. Hook next lp of right-hand strip and pull through lp on hook. Catch next lp of left-hand strip

and pull through lp on hook. Continue joining lps, alternating right and left strips. Fasten off with sl st.

To join next strip, beg with bottom right lp of left hand strip and join in same manner as first two strips.

Note: *If you do not alternate the beg side in this manner, the top and bottom edges of scarf will be slanted instead of even.*

HAT
STRIPS
Set adjustable loom at 2½-inches wide, make 1 strip 20 sts long, 1 strip 40 sts long, 1 strip 80 sts long and 1 strip 160 sts long.

JOINING STRIPS

Lay 20-st strip and 40-st strip next to each other on flat surface. Beg with 20-st strip and insert hook through bottom left lp of strip; hook right bottom 2 lps of 40-st strip and pull through lp on hook. Hook next lp of 20-st strip and pull through 2 lps on hook. Continue joining in same manner, alternating 2 lps from longer strip with 1 lp from shorter strip. Fasten off with sl st.

Place 80-st strip next to 40-st strip and join as first 2 strips, alternating 1 lp from shorter strip with 2 lps of longer strip.

Place 160-st strip next to 80-st strip and join in same manner.

Insert piece of yarn through all lps on unjoined edge of 20-st strip. Pull tight, drawing joined strips into a circle. Tie ends to secure.

Sew ends of center sts tog to close rest of circle.

EDGE

Attach yarn through any 2 unjoined lps on outer edge.

Rnd 1: Ch 1, *draw up lp in each of next 2 lps, yo and draw through all 3 lps on hook; rep from * around; join in first sc. *(80 sc)*

Note: For **sec dec,** *draw up lp in each of next 2 sts indicated, yo and draw through all 3 lps on hook.*

Rnd 2: Ch 1, *sc in next sc, **sc dec** (see Note) in next 2 sc; rep from * to last 2 sc; sc in last 2 sc; join in first sc. *(54 sc)*

Rnd 3: Ch 1, sc in each sc; join in first sc.

Fasten off and weave in all ends.

ADJUSTING FOR INDIVIDUAL FIT

At end of rnd 2, test for fit. If hat needs to be smaller, determine how much smaller, then dec (evenly spaced) the appropriate additional number of sts on rnd 3, working even thereafter.

If you need a larger fit, determine how much larger you need to make the edge. Remove rnd 2, and rework it with the necessary number fewer dec (evenly spaced) to get the size you need. Work even thereafter. ❧

Quick Chullo Hat

DESIGN BY MARIA MERLINO

SKILL LEVEL ◼◼▢▢
EASY

FINISHED SIZE
Approximately 20 inches in circumference

MATERIALS
 Lion Brand Jiffy Thick & Quick super bulky (super chunky) weight yarn
    5 oz/84 yds/140g #207 green mountains
- Size N/15/10mm crochet hook or size needed to obtain gauge
- Tapestry needle

GAUGE
4 sts = 2 inches

PATTERN NOTE
Hat is worked in continuous rounds; do not join. Mark beginning of rounds.

Instructions

HAT
Rnd 1: Ch 2, 6 sc in 2nd ch from hook. *(6 sts)*

Rnd 2: [2 sc in front lp of next st, 2 sc in back lp of next st] 3 times. *(12 sts)*

Rnd 3: [Sc in back lp of next st, 2 sc in front lp of next st] 6 times. *(18 sts)*

Rnd 4: [Sc in front lp of next st, sc in back lp of next st, 2 sc in front lp of next st, sc in back lp of next st, sc in front lp of next st, 2 sc in back lp of next st] 3 times. *(24 sts)*

Rnd 5: [Sc in back lp of next st, sc in front lp of next st, sc in back lp of next st, 2 sc in front lp of next st] 6 times. *(30 sts)*

Rnd 6: [Sc in front lp of next st, sc in back lp of next st, sc in front lp of next st, sc in back lp of next st, 2 sc in front lp of next st, sc in back lp of next st, sc in front lp of next st, sc in back lp of next st, sc in front lp of next st, 2 sc in back lp of next st] 3 times. *(36 sts)*

Rnds 7–11: Sc in each st.

Do not fasten off.

FIRST EAR FLAP
Row 1: Working in **front lps** only, sc in each of next 12 sts, turn. *(12 sts)*

Row 2: Ch 1, sk first sc, [sc in front lp of next st, sc in back lp of next st] 5 times, sc in front lp of next st, turn. *(11 sts)*

Row 3: Sk first sc, [sc in back lp of next st, sc in front lp of next st] 5 times, turn. *(10 sts)*

Row 4: Sk first sc, [sc in back lp of next st, sc in front lp of next st] 4 times, sc in back lp of next st, turn. *(9 sts)*

Row 5: Sk first sc, [sc in back lp of next st, sc in front lp of next st] 4 times, turn. *(8 sts)*

Row 6: Sk first sc, [sc in back lp of next st, sc in front lp of next st] 3 times, sc in back lp of next st, turn. *(7 sts)*

Row 7: Sk first sc, [sc in back lp of next st, sc in front lp of next st] 3 times, turn. *(6 sts)*

Row 8: Sk first sc, [sc in back lp of next st, sc in front lp of next st] twice, sc in back lp of next st, turn. *(5 sts)*

Row 9: Sk first sc, [sc in back lp of next st, sc in front lp of next st] twice, turn. *(4 sts)*

Row 10: Sk first sc, sc in back lp of next st, sc in front lp of next st, sc in back lp of next st, turn. *(3 sts)*

Row 11: Sc in front lp of next st, sc in back lp of next st, turn. *(2 sts)*

Row 12: Sk first sc, sc in back lp of next st, turn. *(1 st)*

Row 13: Sl st in first sc, ch 21, draw up a 3-inch length. Fasten off. Fluff out the 3-inch end.

SECOND EAR FLAP

Sk next 8 sts from First Ear Flap, attach yarn with a sl st in next st.

Rep rows 1–13 of First Ear Flap. 🌱

Just Peachy Set

DESIGN BY JACQUELINE STETTER

SKILL LEVEL ◖■□□
EASY

FINISHED SIZES
Scarf: Approximately 58 inches long x
5 inches wide
Hat: 25 inches in circumference

MATERIALS

Red Heart Soft Baby light (light worsted)
weight yarn:
7 oz/575 yds/198g #7321 powder yellow *(A)*
Red Heart Tiki medium (worsted) weight yarn:
5⅖ oz/471 yds/150g #3260 peach *(B)*
Moda Dea Cheri medium (worsted) weight yarn:
1¾ oz/81 yds/50g #9257 orange *(C)*
Size I/9/5.5mm crochet hook or size needed to
    obtain gauge
Tapestry needle

GAUGE
4 hdc = 1 inch; 4 rows = 2 inches

PATTERN NOTES
Scarf is reversible.

Join with slip stitch unless otherwise stated.

Instructions

SCARF
Row 1: With 1 strand each of A and B held tog,
ch 22, hdc in 2nd ch from hook and in each rem ch
across, turn. *(20 sts)*

Row 2: Ch 2, hdc in each hdc across, turn.

Rep row 2 until scarf measures approximately
58 inches, changing to C in last st, turn.

EDGING
Row 1: Ch 3, dc in each hdc across, turn.

Row 2: Ch 2, hdc in each dc across, turn.

Rows 3–6: [Rep rows 1 and 2] twice. Fasten off.

Rep edging on opposite end of scarf.

Weave in all ends.

HAT
Rnd 1: With 1 strand each of A and B held tog,
ch 4, sl st in first ch to form ring, ch 3, 11 dc in ring,
join with sl st in top of ch-3. *(12 sts)*

Rnd 2: Ch 3, dc in first st, 2 dc in each st around,
join in top of ch-3. *(24 sts)*

Rnd 3: Ch 2, hdc in first st, hdc in next st, [2 hdc in
next st, hdc in next st] around, join. *(36 sts)*

Rnd 4: Ch 3, dc in first st, dc in next 2 sts [2 dc in
next st, dc in next 2 sts] around, join. *(48 sts)*

Rnd 5: Ch 2, hdc in first st, ch 1 [hdc in next 4 sts,
ch 1] 11 times, hdc in next 3 sts, join in first hdc.
(48 sts, 12 ch-1 sps)

Rnd 6: Ch 3, [2 dc in next ch-1 sp, dc in next 4 sts] 11 times, 2 dc in next ch-1 sp, dc in next 3 st, join top of ch-3. *(72 sts)*

Rnd 7: Ch 2, hdc in same st, hdc in each st around, join.

Rnds 8–14: Ch 3, dc in next st and in each st around, join.

Rnd 15: Ch 3, dc in next st and in each st around, changing to C in last st, turn.

Rnds 16–19: Ch 2, hdc in each st around, join.

Rnd 20: Ch 3, dc in each st around, join.

Rnd 21: Ch 2, hdc in each st around. Fasten off, leaving long tail.

FINISHING

Fold rnds 16–21 back to make hatband. Weave long tail through rnd 21 and body of hat to hold band in place.

Weave in all ends. ❧

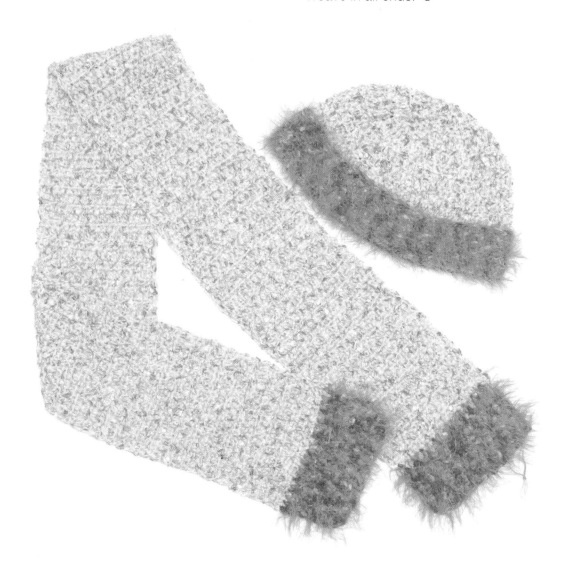

Wardrobe Warming Scarf

DESIGN BY ZELDA WORKMAN

SKILL LEVEL
EASY

FINISHED SIZE
Approximately 35 inches across neck edge x
17 inches from neck edge to point.

MATERIALS
Patons Carmen bulky (chunky) weight yarn:
3½ oz/128 yds/98g #07013 chocolate
Size M/13/9mm crochet hook or size needed
   to obtain gauge
Tapestry needle

GAUGE
Rows 1–3 = 3 inches high x 4½ inches wide

SPECIAL STITCHES
Beginning V-stitch (beg V-st): Ch 4, dc in first dc.

V-stitch (V-st): In st or sp indicated work (dc, ch 1, dc).

Instructions

SCARF
Row 1: Ch 5, dc in 5th ch from hook, turn. *(1 V-st)*

Row 2: Beg V-st *(see Special Stitches)*, ch 1, sk next ch, **V-st** *(see Special Stitches)* in next ch, turn. *(2 V-sts)*

Row 3: Beg V-st, ch 1, V-st in ch-1 sp between V-sts, ch 1, V-st in 3rd ch of beg ch-4, turn. *(3 V-sts)*

Rows 4–16: Beg V-st, [ch 1, V-st in ch-1 between V-sts] to last ch-1, V-st in 3rd ch of beg ch-4, turn. Do not turn at end of row 16. *(16 V-sts)*

EDGING
Working along side edge of scarf toward point, sc around edge dc [ch 3, sc around edge dc of next row] to end of row 1, ch 3, sc in opposite end of row 1, [ch 3, sc around edge dc of next row] to end of row 16, [ch 3, sc in center of V-st, ch 3, sc in ch-1 between V-sts] to end of row 16, ch 3, sl st in top of first sc.

Fasten off and weave in all ends. ❧

Watercolor Impressions Set

DESIGN BY DARLA FANTON

SKILL LEVEL ◼◼◼◻ INTERMEDIATE

FINISHED SIZE
Hat: 23 inches in circumference
Scarf: 6½ x 70 inches

MATERIALS

 Lion Brand Homespun bulky (chunky) weight yarn:
7½ oz/232 yds/210g each #309 deco *(A)* and #315 tudor *(B)*

 Lion Brand Fun Fur Prints bulky (chunky) weight eyelash yarn (optional):
1¾ oz/67 yds/49g #205 sandstone *(C)*
Size K/10½/6.5mm double-ended crochet hook or size needed to obtain gauge
Size K/10½/6.5mm crochet hook or size needed to obtain gauge (optional)
Tapestry needle

GAUGE
In pattern 3 sts = 1 inch; 5 rows = 1 inch

SPECIAL STITCH
Knit stitch (K): Insert hook between front and back bars of indicated vertical st, yo and draw through keeping lp on hook.

Instructions

HAT
Note: *Hat is worked from bottom up.*

Row 1: With A ch 66, working in **back lps** *(see Stitch Guide)* only, insert hook in 2nd ch from hook, yo and draw through, forming lp on hook; *insert hook in next ch, yo and draw through; rep from * across. Slide all lps to opposite end of hook and turn. *(66 lps on hook)*

Row 2: To work lps off hook, with B make slip knot on hook, working left to right, draw lp through first lp on hook; *yo, draw through 2 lps *(1 of each color)*, rep from * until 1 lp remains on hook. Do not turn.

Row 3: With B and working right to left, ch 1, sk first vertical bar; *yo, sk next vertical bar, **K** *(see Special Stitch)* in next vertical st; rep from * across, ending K in last vertical st. Slide all sts to opposite end of hook and turn. *(66 lps on hook)*

Row 4: With A, yo and draw through 1 lp; *yo and draw through 2 lps; rep from * until 1 lp remains on hook. Do not turn.

Row 5: Rep row 3 with A.

Row 6: Rep row 4 with B.

Rows 7–28: Rep rows 3–6 ending with a row 4.

CROWN SHAPING
Row 29: With A, ch 1, sk first vertical bar; *[yo, sk next vertical bar, K in next vertical st] 7 times; sk next vertical bar, K in next vertical st; rep from * across, ending K in last vertical st. Slide all sts to opposite end of hook and turn. *(62 lps on hook)*

Row 30: Rep row 6.

Row 31: With B, ch 1, sk first vertical bar, *[yo, sk next vertical bar, K in next vertical st] 6 times, sk next vertical bar, K in next vertical st; rep from *

Row 37: With A, ch 1, sk first vertical bar, *[yo, sk next vertical bar, K in next vertical st] 5 times, sk next vertical bar, K in next vertical st; rep from * across, ending K in last vertical st. Slide all sts to opposite end of hook and turn. *(46 lps on hook)*

Row 38: Rep row 6.

Row 39: With B, ch 1, sk first vertical bar. *[yo, sk next vertical bar, K in next vertical st] 4 times, sk next vertical bar, K in next vertical st; rep from * 3 times more, [yo, sk next vertical bar, K in next vertical st] twice, K in last vertical st. Slide all sts to opposite end of hook and turn. *(42 lps on hook)*

Row 40: Rep row 4.

Row 41: With A, ch 1, sk first vertical bar, *[yo, sk next vertical bar, K in next vertical st] 4 times, sk next vertical bar, K in next vertical st; rep from * across, ending K in last vertical st. Slide all sts to opposite end of hook and turn. *(38 lps on hook)*

Row 42: Rep row 6.

Row 43: With B, ch 1, sk first vertical bar, *[yo, sk next vertical bar, K in next vertical st] 3 times, sk next vertical bar, K in next vertical st; rep from * 3 times more, [yo, sk next vertical bar, K in next vertical st] twice, K in last vertical st. Slide all sts to opposite end of hook and turn. *(34 lps on hook)*

Row 44: Rep row 4.

Row 45: With A, ch 1, sk first vertical bar, *[yo, sk next vertical bar, K in next vertical st] 3 times, sk next vertical bar, K in next vertical st; rep from * across, ending K in last vertical st. Slide all sts to opposite end of hook and turn. *(30 lps on hook)*

Row 46: Rep row 6.

Row 47: With B, ch 1, sk first vertical bar, *[yo, sk next vertical bar, K in next vertical st] twice, sk next vertical bar, K in next vertical st; rep from * across, K in last vertical st. Slide all sts to opposite end of hook and turn. *(26 lps on hook)*

Row 48: Rep row 4.

Row 49: Rep row 47 with A. *(22 lps on hook)*

Row 50: Rep row 6.

3 times more, [yo, sk next vertical bar, K in next vertical st] twice, K in last vertical st. Slide all sts to opposite end of hook and turn. *(58 lps on hook)*

Row 32: Rep row 4.

Row 33: With A, ch 1, sk first vertical bar, *[yo, sk next vertical bar, K in next vertical st] 6 times, sk next vertical bar, K in next vertical st; rep from * across, ending K in last vertical st. Slide all sts to opposite end of hook and turn. *(54 lps on hook)*

Row 34: Rep row 6.

Row 35: With B, ch 1, sk first vertical st, *[yo, sk next vertical bar, K in next vertical st] 5 times, sk next vertical bar, K in next vertical st; rep from * 3 times more, [yo, sk next vertical bar, K in next vertical st] twice, K in last vertical st. Slide all sts to opposite end of hook and turn. *(50 lps on hook)*

Row 36: Rep row 4.

Row 51: With B, ch 1, sk first vertical bar, *yo, [sk next vertical bar, K in next vertical st] twice; rep from * across, ending K in last vertical st. Slide all sts to opposite end of hook and turn. *(17 lps on hook)*

Row 52: Rep row 4.

Row 53: With A, ch 1, sk first vertical bar; *K in next vertical st, sk next vertical bar; rep from * across, ending K in last vertical st. *(10 lps on hook)*

FINISHING

Fasten off B. Cut A, leaving a 20-inch end. With tapestry needle, thread end through rem sts and pull tight; continue sewing center back seam with whipstitch. Fasten off and weave in all ends.

OPTIONAL EYELASH TRIM

Note: *On rows 2 and 3, folding the work along row you are working on will make the sts easier to locate and work into. You are working hdc as a surface st that will show only on one side.*

Row 1: With eyelash yarn and regular hook and working in opposite side of foundation ch with predominantly A side facing, join with sl st in first ch; ch 2; hdc in each ch across, join with sl st in top of beg ch-2, turn.

Row 2: Continue working with predominantly A side facing you, ch 2, sk B rows, working in **front lp** *(see Stitch Guide)* of A color horizontal sts, hdc in each st across, turn.

Row 3: Rep row 2.

Fasten off and weave in all ends.

SCARF
Row 1: With A ch 18; working in back lps only, pick up lp in 2nd ch from hook; *pick up lp in next ch; rep from * across beg ch, leaving all lps on hook. Slide all sts to opposite end of hook and turn. *(18 lps on hook)*

Row 2: To work lps off hook, with B make sl knot on hook, working from left to right draw slip knot through first lp; *yo, draw through 2 lps (1 lp of each color); rep from * until 1 lp remains on hook. Do not turn.

Row 3: With B and working right to left, ch 1, sk first vertical bar; *yo, sk next vertical bar, K in next vertical st; rep from * across, ending K in last vertical st. Slide all sts to opposite end of hook and turn. *(18 lps on hook)*

Row 4: With A, yo and draw through 1 lp; * yo and draw through 2 lps; rep from * until 1 lp remains on hook. Do not turn.

Row 5: Rep row 3 with A.

Row 6: Rep row 4 with B.

Rows 7–337: Rep rows 3–6, ending with a row 4.

Row 338: Bind off in following manner: with A, ch 1, sk first vertical bar; *sl st under next vertical bar; rep from * across.

Fasten off and weave in all ends.

OPTIONAL EYELASH TRIM
Row 1: With C, regular hook and working in opposite side of beg ch with predominantly A side facing you, join with sl st in first ch; ch 2; hdc in each ch across.

Row 2: Continue working with predominantly A side facing you, ch 2, sk B rows, working in **front lp** of A color horizontal sts, hdc in each st across.

Row 3: Rep row 2.

Fasten off and weave in all ends.

Rep trim for opposite end of scarf, beg in row 338. ❦

Marvelous Möbius Scarf

DESIGN BY NAZANIN FARD

SKILL LEVEL EASY

FINISHED SIZE
15 inches wide x 45 inches around

MATERIALS
 Moda Dea Chichi bulky (chunky) weight yarn:
8¾ oz/435 yds/ 245g #9948 funky
Size I/9/5.5 mm crochet hook
Tapestry needle

GAUGE
10 dc = 4 inches

Instructions

MOEBIUS
Note: *Be careful to work every st available, especially the last st of the row.*

RIBBING
Row 1 (RS): Ch 52, dc in 3rd ch from hook and in each rem ch, turn. *(50 sts)*

Row 2: Ch 2, dc in each dc, turn.

Rep row 2, until piece measures approximately 45 inches. Fasten off. Do not cut yarn.

FINISHING
Referring to Fig. 1, sew the beg and end of the scarf tog.

Weave in all ends. 🌱

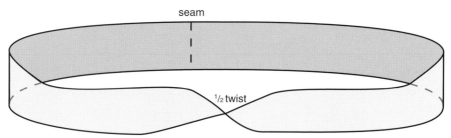

seam

½ twist

Fig. 1

Comfort in the Furry Hood

DESIGN BY TAMMY HILDEBRAND

SKILL LEVEL ◧■◻◻
EASY

FINISHED SIZE
One size fits most

MATERIALS
 Bernat Boa bulky (chunky) weight yarn:
6½ oz/252 yds/182g #81307 emu
Size P/15/10mm crochet hook or size needed
to obtain gauge
Tapestry needle

GAUGE
3 sc and 2 ch-1 sps in pattern = 3 inches;
4 rows = 3 inches

Pattern Notes
Piece is worked with 2 strands of yarn held
together throughout.

Join with slip stitch unless otherwise noted.

Instructions

SCARF
Rnd 1 (RS): Beg at neck, ch 40, join to form a ring,
ch 1, sc in each ch, join in first sc. *(40 sc)*

Rnd 2: Ch 1, sc in first st, ch 1, sk next st [sc in next
st, ch 1, sk next st] 19 times, join in first sc. *(20 sc)*

Rnds 3–21: Ch 1, sc in first st, ch 1, sk next ch-1
sp, [sc in next st, ch 1, sk next ch-1 sp] 19 times,
join in first sc.

HOOD
Row 1: Ch 1, sc in first st, [ch 1, sk next ch-1 sp,
sc in next st] 13 times, turn, leaving rem sts
unworked. *(14 sc)*

Rows 2–12: Ch 1, sc in first st, [ch 1, sk next ch-1
sp, sc in next st] 13 times, turn.

Row 13: Ch 1, sk first st and first ch-1 sp, sc in next
st, [ch 1, sk next ch-1 sp, sc in next st] 11 times,
turn. *(12 sc)*

Row 14: Ch 1, sk first st and ch-1 sp, sc in next
st, [ch 1, sk next ch-1 sp, sc in next st] 9 times,
turn. *(10 sc)*

Rows 15 & 16: Ch 1, sc in first st, [ch 1, sk next ch-
1 sp, sc in next st] 9 times, turn.

Row 17: Ch 1, sc in first st, [ch 1, sk next ch-1 sp,
sc in next st] 9 times. Do not turn.

FACE OPENING
Note: *For **dec**, [yo, pull up lp in next st] twice, yo
and draw through all 3 lps on hook.*

Rnd 1: Ch 1, sc in end st of rows 1–17, ch 1,
working in unworked sts of rnd 21, [sc in next st,
ch 1, sk next ch-1 sp] 6 times, sc in edge sts of
rows 1–17 of opposite side. *(40 sc)*

Rnd 2: [Dec *(see note)* in next 2 sts] 13 times, sc
in next st, ch 1, sk next ch-1 sp, [sc in next st, ch 1,
sk next ch-1 sp] 6 times, sc in next st [dec in next 2
sts] 8 times, join. *(29 sc)*

Rnd 3: Ch 1, sc in next 14 sts, ch 1, [sc in next st,
ch 1, sk next ch-1 sp] 6 times, sc in last 9 sts, join.
Fasten off and weave in all ends. ❧

Babette Hat & Scarf

DESIGN BY JOY PRESCOTT

SKILL LEVEL INTERMEDIATE

FINISHED SIZES
Instructions given fit child size 4; changes for child sizes 6 and 8 are in [ ].

FINISHED GARMENT MEASUREMENT
Hat: 16 [17, 18] inches in circumference
Scarf: 4½ inches x 33 [35, 37] inches.

MATERIALS
 Lion Brand Baby fine (sport) weight yarn:
3¼ oz/300 yds/92g [3⅘ oz/350 yds/107g, 4⅜ oz/400 yds/123g] #143 lavender *(A)*
 Paton's Twister super bulky (super chunky) weight yarn:
1¾ oz/50 yds/50g [2 oz/55 yds/58g, 2¼ oz/60 yds/64g] #05711 fruit loops *(B)*
Size P/15/10mm crochet hook or size needed to obtain gauge
Tapestry needle

GAUGE
9 pat sts = 4 inches; 7 rows/rnds = 2 inches

PATTERN NOTE
Join each round with slip stitch unless otherwise noted.

SPECIAL STITCHES
Pattern stitch (pat st): Insert hook in same sp as previous st, draw up a lp, draw up a lp in next 2 sts, yo and draw through all 4 lps on hook, ch 1.

Modified pattern stitch (modified pat st): Insert hook in next st, draw up a lp, draw up a lp in next 2 sts, yo and draw through all 4 lps on hook, ch 1.

Instructions

HAT
With A ch 60 [64, 68], join to form a ring.

Rnd 1: Ch 1, sc in first st, work in **pat st** *(see Special Stitches)* around, turn. *(29 [31, 33] pat sts)*

Rnd 2: Ch 1, sc in first st, work in pat st around, turn.

Rnds 3–14 [16, 18]: Rep rnd 2.

Rnds 15 [17, 19]: Ch 1, work 5 [6, 7] pat sts, *ch 5, sk 5 pat sts *, work 10 pat sts, rep from * to * once, work 4 [5, 6] pat sts. *(19 [21, 23] pat sts)*

Rnd 16 [18, 20]: Ch 1, work in **modified pat sts** *(see Special Stitches)* around. *(13 [15, 17] pat sts)*

Rnd 17 [19, 21]: Rep rnd 16 [18, 20]. *(8 [10, 13] pat sts)*

Rnd 18 [20, 22]: Work even in pat st.

Rnds 19 & 20 [21 & 22, 23 & 24]: Rep rnd 16 [18, 20].

Fasten off leaving a 10-inch end for sewing.

With tapestry needle and long end, catch rem sts. Pull tight to close opening, knot and weave in all ends.

TUBE

Rnd 1: Working in first opening, join A with sl st in same sp as last worked on Rnd 15 [17, 19], ch 1, pat st around. *(9 pat sts)*

Work even for 27 [29, 31] rnds.

Fasten off leaving a 10-inch end for sewing.

With tapestry needle and long end, sew end of tube to other opening on hat.

TIE

With B, ch 35, sc in 2nd ch from hook and in each rem ch across. Fasten off. Tie to center of tube.

BOTTOM TRIM

Note: For **dec**, [yo, pull up lp in next st] twice, yo and draw through all 3 lps on hook.

Rnd 1: Join B with sl st in any st along beg ch and work 54 [55, 56] sc evenly spaced around.

Rnds 2–5: Sc in each st around.

Rnd 6: *Sc in next 2 sts, **dec** *(see note)* in next 2 sts; rep from * around, sc in last 2 sts. *(41 [42, 43] sts)*

SCARF

Row 1: With A, ch 23, sc in 2nd ch from hook, work pat st to last st, sc in last st.

Rows 2–104 [111, 118]: Ch 1, sc in first st, pat st to last st, sc in last st, turn. At end of last row, do not turn.

Fasten off and weave in all ends.

FINISHING

Row 1: Join B with sl st in first st, ch 1, work 14 sc evenly spaced across, turn.

Rows 2–5: Sc in each st across.

Fasten off and weave in all ends.

Rep rows 1–5 on other end of scarf. ❦

Keep-the-Chill-Out Leg Warmers

DESIGN BY JOY PRESCOTT

SKILL LEVEL

FINISHED SIZES
Instructions given fit child size; changes for adult size are in [ ].

FINISHED GARMENT MEASUREMENT
Child size: approximately 11½ inches long x 9 inches in top circumference
Adult size: approximately 14 inches long x 11 inches in top circumference

MATERIALS
 Caron Jewel Box medium (worsted) weight yarn:
    4½ oz/180 yds/126g [6¾ oz/270 yds/189g]
    #0020 ruby [#0002 moonstone]
Size G/6/4mm [H/8/5mm] crochet hook or size needed to obtain gauge
Tapestry needle

GAUGE
4 rnds = 2 inches; 7 sts = 2 inches

SPECIAL STITCH
Tall half double crochet (tall hdc): Yo, insert hook in st indicated, draw up lp, yo and draw through 1 lp on hook, yo and draw through all 3 lps on hook.

Instructions

LEG WARMER
RIBBING
Row 1 (RS): Ch 11 [13], sc in 2nd ch from hook and in each ch, turn. *(10 [12] sc)*

Row 2: Ch 1, working in **back lps** *(see Stitch Guide)* only, sc in each sc, turn.

Rows 3–30 [36]: Rep row 2.

Next row: Holding first and last rows of ribbing tog, sl st in back lps of each row to join ribbing. Turn piece inside out so that sl st joining is on WS.

BODY
Note: *Join with sl st unless otherwise noted.*

Rnd 1: Ch 3, working along sides of ribbing in ends of rows, work **tall hdc** *(see Special Stitch)* in end of each row around ribbing, join with sl st in top of beg ch-3, turn. *(30 [36] sts)*

Rnds 2–11 [12]: Ch 3, tall hdc in each st, join, turn.

For Child Size Only
Rnd 12: Ch 3, *tall hdc in next 4 sts, 2 tall hdc in next st; rep from * around, join, turn. *(36 sts)*

Rnd 13: Ch 3, tall hdc in each st, join, turn.

Rnd 14: Ch 3, *tall hdc in next 5 sts, 2 tall hdc in next st; rep from * around, join, turn. *(42 sts)*

Rnd 15: Ch 3, tall hdc in each st, join, turn.

Rnd 16: Ch 1, **reverse sc** *(see Stitch Guide)* in each st.

Fasten off and weave in all ends.

For Adult Size Only
Rnd 13: Ch 3, *tall hdc in next 5 sts, 2 tall hdc in next st; rep from * around, join, turn. *(42 sts)*

Rnd 14: Ch 3, tall hdc in each st, join, turn.

Rnd 15: Ch 3, *tall hdc in next 6 sts, 2 tall hdc in next st; rep from *around, join, turn. *(48 sts)*

Rnd 16: Ch 3, tall hdc in each st, join, turn.

Rnd 17: Ch 3, *tall hdc in next 7 sts, 2 tall hdc in next st; rep from * around, join, turn. *(54 sts)*

Rnds 18–19: Ch 3, tall hdc in each st, join, turn.

Rnd 20: Ch 1, **reverse sc** *(see Stitch Guide)* in each st around.

Fasten off and weave in all ends.

EDGING
Note: *For **dec**, draw up lp in each of next 2 sts, yo and draw through all 3 lps on hook.*

Join yarn with sl st in end of any row at top of leg warmer ribbing, ch 1, *sc in next 4 sts, **dec** *(see Note)* in next 2 sts; rep from * around. *(25 [30] sts)*

Fasten off and weave in all ends. ❦

Sensuous Wraps

When you need something to warm your
shoulders, look to this fashionable selection.
These shawls, ponchos, ponchettes and
capelets are definitely not your usual cardigan.

Get Together for Popcorn Ponchos

DESIGN BY JACQUELINE STETTER

Mother Poncho

SKILL LEVEL ■□□□
BEGINNER

FINISHED SIZE
Panel: 19 x 32 inches

MATERIALS

 Red Heart Plush medium (worsted) weight yarn:
24 oz/1160 yds/672g #9220 apricot *(A)*

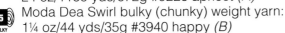 Moda Dea Swirl bulky (chunky) weight yarn:
1¼ oz/44 yds/35g #3940 happy *(B)*
Size I/9/5.5mm crochet hook or size needed to obtain gauge
Tapestry needle

GAUGE
16 hdc = 5 inches; 16 rows = 6 inches

Instructions

PANEL A
Row 1 (RS): With A, ch 60, sc in 2nd ch from hook and in each rem ch, turn. *(59 sc)*

Row 2: Ch 1, sc in first sc, [tr in next sc, sc in next sc] across, turn.

Row 3: Ch 1, sc in each st across, turn. *(59 sc)*

Rep rows 2 and 3, until panel measures approximately 32 inches from beg, ending with a row 3.

Fasten off, leaving a 40-inch length for sewing panels tog.

PANEL B
Work same as Panel A.

ASSEMBLY
Referring to Fig. 1 for placement, with tapestry needle, sew the end of Panel A to the side of Panel B, then sew the end of Panel B to the side of Panel A.

NECK EDGING
Rnd 1: Join B with sc in back V of neck, sc evenly around neck edge, join with sl st in first sc.

Rnd 2: Ch 1, sc in each sc around, join. Fasten off.

JOINING TRIM & LOWER EDGING
Referring to photo for placement, join B with sc at neck edge of front seam, sc around posts along seam to lower edge. Do not fasten off.

Rnd 1: Ch 1, sc evenly around lower edge, join in first sc.

Rnd 2: Ch 1, sc in each sc around, join in first sc.

Rnd 3: Rep rnd 2.

Fasten off and weave in all ends.

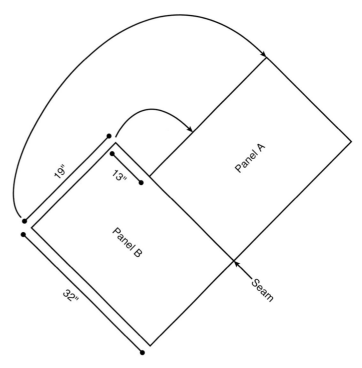

Fig. 1

Daughter Poncho

SKILL LEVEL ◼□□□
BEGINNER

FINISHED SIZE
Panel: 14½ x 23 inches

MATERIALS
4 Red Heart Plush medium (worsted)
MEDIUM weight yarn:
12 oz/580 yds/336g #9822 bluebird *(A)*
5 Moda Dea Swirl bulky (chunky) weight yarn:
BULKY 1 oz/35 yds/28g #3940 happy *(B)*
Size I/9/5.5mm crochet hook or size needed to
obtain gauge
Tapestry needle

GAUGE
16 hdc = 5 inches; 16 rows = 6 inches

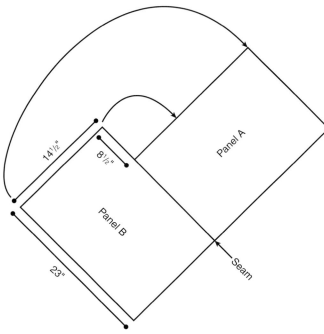

Fig. 2

Instructions

PANEL A
Row 1 (RS): With A, ch 44, sc in 2nd ch from hook and in each rem ch, turn. *(43 sc)*

Row 2: Ch 1, sc in first sc, [tr in next sc, sc in next sc] across, turn.

Row 3: Ch 1, sc in each st across, turn. *(43 sc)*

Rep rows 2 and 3, until panel measures approximately 23 inches from beg, ending with a row 3.

Fasten off, leaving a 30-inch length for sewing panels tog.

PANEL B
Work same as Panel A.

ASSEMBLY
Referring to Fig. 2 for placement, with tapestry needle, sew the end of Panel A to the side of Panel B, then sew the end of Panel B to the side of Panel A.

NECK EDGING
Rnd 1: Join B with sc in back V of neck, work sc evenly spaced around neck edge, join with sl st in first sc.

Rnd 2: Ch 1, sc in each sc around, join. Fasten off.

JOINING TRIM & LOWER EDGING
Referring to photo for placement, join B with sc at neck edge of front seam, sc around posts along seam to lower edge. Do not fasten off.

Rnd 1: Ch 1, sc evenly around lower edge, join in first sc.

Rnd 2: Ch 1, sc in each sc around, join.

Rnd 3: Rep rnd 2.

Fasten off and weave in all ends. ❧

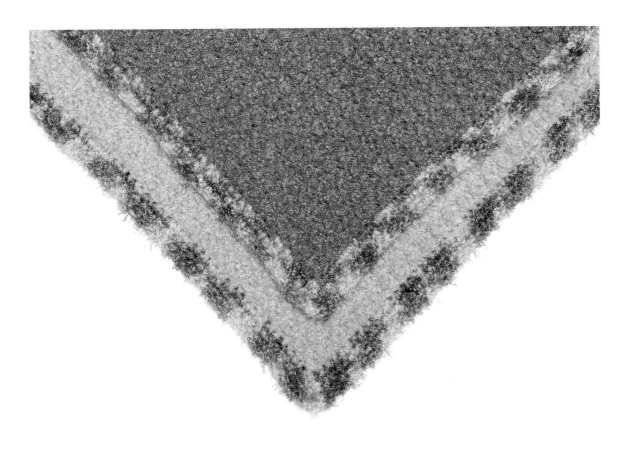

Wrap-Yourself-Up Lush Shawl

DESIGN BY ZELDA WORKMAN

SKILL LEVEL ◖■□□
EASY

FINISHED SIZE
Approximately 27 x 87 inches

MATERIALS
 Patons Carmen bulky (chunky) weight yarn: 1¾ oz/64 yds/50g #07310 violet
Size M/13/9mm crochet hook or size needed to obtain gauge
Tapestry needle

GAUGE
6 V-sts = 9 inches

SPECIAL STITCH
V-stitch (V-st): In st or sp indicated work (dc, ch 1, dc).

Instructions

SHAWL
Row 1 (RS): Ch 47, sc in 2nd ch from hook and in each ch across, turn. *(46 sc)*

Row 2: Ch 3 *(counts as dc)*, sk first sc, dc in next sc, sk next sc, **V-st** *(see Special Stitch)* in next sc, sk next 2 sc, rep from * to last 3 sc, sk next sc, dc in last 2 sc, turn. *(14 V-sts)*

Row 3: Ch 3, sk first dc, dc in next dc, *V-st in ch-1 sp of next V-st, rep from * to last 2 dc, dc in last 2 dc, turn. *(14 V-sts)*

Rep row 3 until piece measures approximately 78 inches, ending with a RS row, turn.

Next row (WS): Ch 1, sc in each st across, turn. *(46 sc)*

Do not fasten off.

EDGING
Rnd 1 (RS): Ch 1, sc in first sc, [ch 3, sk next 2 sc, sc in next sc] across; working along next side in sps formed by edge st, [ch 3, sc in next sp] across; ch 3, working in unused lps of beg ch, sc in first lp [ch 3, sk next 2 lps, sc in next lp] across; working along next side in sps formed by edge st, [ch 3, sc in next sp] across, join with sl st in first sc.

Rnd 2: [Ch 3, sc in next ch-3 sp] around. Do not join. Mark last ch-3 sp.

Rnds 3–5: [Ch 3, sc in next ch-3 sp] around, marking last ch-3 sp on each rnd. At end of rnd 5, ch 3, sl st in marked ch-3 sp.

Fasten off and weave in all ends.

Soft & Stylish Go-Anywhere Ponchette

DESIGN BY ZELDA WORKMAN

SKILL LEVEL ◼◼◻◻
EASY

FINISHED SIZE
Approximately 19 inches from neck edge to bottom front point

MATERIALS
 Bernat Bling Bling bulky (chunky) weight yarn: 7 oz/360 yds/196g #65244 spotlight sage
Size M/13/9mm crochet hook or size needed to obtain gauge
Tapestry needle
Stitch markers

GAUGE
Rnds 1–3 = 4 inches

PATTERN NOTES
Join with slip stitch unless otherwise stated.

Mark the first stitch of each round and chain-2 increase space on rounds 8–19.

Instructions

PONCHETTE
Rnd 1 (RS): Ch 40, join to form ring being careful not to twist work, ch 1, sc in each ch around, join with sl st in first sc. *(40 sc)*

Rnd 2: Ch 1, [sc, ch 1] in each sc around, join in first sc. *(40 ch-1 sps)*

Rnd 3: Ch 1, [sc, ch 2] in each sc around, join in first sc. *(40 ch-2 sps)*

Rnds 4–7: Ch 1, [sc, ch 3] in each sc around, join in first sc. *(40 ch-3 sps)*

Rnd 8: Sl st to center of next ch-3 sp, ch 1, sc in same sp [ch 3, sc in next sp] twice, ch 3, (hdc, ch 2, hdc) in next sp *(inc),* [ch 3, sc in next sp] to last sp, ch 3, join in first sc. *(40 ch-3 sps and 1 inc sp)*

Rnds 9–11: Rep rnd 8. *(43 ch-3 sps and 1 inc sp)*

Rnd 12: Sl st to center of next ch-3 sp, ch 1, sc in same sp [ch 3, sc in next sp] twice, ch 3, (sc, ch 2, sc) in next sp, [ch 3, sc in next sp] to last sp, ch 3, join in first sc. *(44 ch-3 sps and 1 inc sp)*

Rnds 13 & 14: Rep rnd 8. *(46 ch-3 sps and 1 inc sp)*

Rnd 15: Rep rnd 12. *(47 ch-3 sps and 1 inc sp)*

Rnds 16 & 17: Rep rnd 8. *(49 ch-3 sps and 1 inc sp)*

Rnds 18 & 19: Rep rnd 12. *(51 ch-3 sps and 1 inc sp)*

Fasten off.

NECK EDGE
Working in unused lps of beg ch, join with an sc in any lp, sc in each lp, join in joining sc. *(40 sc)*

Fasten off and weave in all ends.

Foxy Lady Shoulder Wrap

DESIGN BY LAURA GEBHARDT

SKILL LEVEL ◼️◼️◻️◻️
EASY

FINISHED SIZE
Approximately 41 x 11½ inches

MATERIALS
 Bernat Boa bulky (chunky) weight yarn:
12¼ oz/497 yds/343g #81940 chinchilla
Size K/10½/6.5mm crochet hook or size needed to obtain gauge
Tapestry needle
Decorative hook-and-eye closure
Sewing needle and matching thread

GAUGE
11½ sc = 4 inches; 9 rows = 4 inches

Instructions

WRAP
Make 2.

Note: *For **sc dec,** Draw up lp in each of next 2 sts indicated, yo and draw through all 3 lps on hook.*

Row 1 (RS): Ch 8, sc in 2nd ch from hook and in each rem ch, turn. *(7 sc)*

Row 2: Ch 1, sc in each sc to last sc, 2 sc in last sc, turn. *(9 sc)*

Rows 3–27: Rep row 2. *(33 sc)*

Row 28: Ch 1, sc in each sc, turn.

Rep row 28 until piece measures 31 inches from beg.

Next row: Ch 1, sc in each sc to last 2 sts, **sc dec** *(see Note)* over next 2 sts.

Rep last row until 7 sts rem.

Fasten off and weave in all ends.

FINISHING
Place 2 pieces tog with WS facing. Sew around outside edges. Referring to photo for placement, sew hook and eye to opposite short ends of wrap. ❦

Furry Fun Kid's Poncho

DESIGN BY LAURA GEBHARDT

SKILL LEVEL BEGINNER

FINISHED SIZE
Instructions given fit child's size 4–6; changes for size 8–10 are in [ ].

FINISHED MEASUREMENTS
Panel: 14 [21] x 17 [24] inches

MATERIALS
 Moda Dea Dream medium (worsted) weight yarn:
8¾ oz/465 yds/245g [10½ oz/558 yds/294g] #3502 lavender
Size K/10½/6.5mm crochet hook or size needed to obtain gauge
Tapestry needle

GAUGE
11½ hdc = 4 inches; 9 rows = 4 inches

Instructions

PANEL A
Row 1: Ch 42 [50], hdc in 3rd ch from hook *(beg 2 sk chs count as an hdc)* and in each ch across. *(41 [49] hdc)*

Rows 2–49 [56]: Ch 2 *(counts as an hdc throughout),* hdc in each hdc across.

Fasten off and weave in all ends.

PANEL B
Work same as Panel A.

ASSEMBLY
Refer to Fig. 1 for placement. With tapestry needle, sew the end of Panel A to the side of Panel B, then sew the end of Panel B to the side of Panel A. 🐾

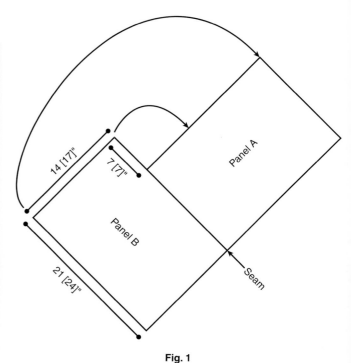

Fig. 1

Paris Stitch Captivating Capelet

DESIGN BY LAURA GEBHARDT

SKILL LEVEL ◖■◻◻ EASY

FINISHED SIZE
Approximately 36 x 19 inches

MATERIALS
6 SUPER BULKY Bernat Galaxy super bulky (super chunky) weight yarn:
  10½ oz/360 yds/294g #53530 Mars
Size K/10½/6.5mm crochet hook or size needed to obtain gauge
Tapestry needle
1-inch diameter button
Sewing needle and matching thread

GAUGE
3 pattern reps = 4 inches; 5½ rows = 4 inches

SPECIAL STITCH
Paris stitch (pst): In st or sp indicated work (2 dc, ch 2, sc).

Instructions

CAPELET
Row 1 (RS): Ch 79, (dc, ch 2, sc) in 3rd ch from hook *(beg 2 sk chs count as a dc)*, *sk next 2 chs, **pst** *(see Special Stitch)* in next ch; rep from * across, turn. *(26 pst)*

Row 2: Ch 3, (dc, ch 2, sc) in next ch-2 sp, pst in each ch-2 sp across, turn.

Rep row 2 until piece measures approximately 18 inches. Fasten off.

EDGING
Hold piece with RS of row 1 at top, join yarn in first ch-2 sp on row 1, ch 3, (dc, ch 2, sc) in same ch, *sk next 2 chs, pst in next ch, rep from * across.

Fasten off and weave in all ends.

FINISHING
Sew button to top left corner. Use ch-2 sp at top right corner as buttonhole. ❦

Adult's Sweater

BACK

Row 1 (RS): Ch 53 [57, 63, 67], hdc in 2nd ch from hook and each ch across, turn. (*51 [55, 61, 65] sts*)

Row 2: Ch 2 (*counts as an hdc*), *ch 1, sk next hdc, hdc in next st, rep from * across, turn.

Row 3: Ch 2, hdc in each ch-1 sp and in each hdc across, turn.

Rows 4 & 5: Ch 2, hdc in each st across, turn.

Rep Rows 2–5.

Note: *Remainder of back is worked in hdc only.*

Work even in hdc until piece measures 10¾ [11¼, 11¾, 12½] inches from beg.

ARMHOLE SHAPING

Sl st in first 5 [6, 7, 7] sts, ch 2 (*counts as an hdc*), hdc in each to last 4 [5, 6, 6] sts, turn. (*43 [45, 49, 53] sts*)

Work even until piece measures 18½ (19½, 20½, 21½] inches from beg, ending with a WS row, turn.

SHOULDER SHAPING

Row 1 (RS): Ch 2, hdc in next 15 [16, 18, 20] sts, turn.

Row 2: Sl st in first 6 sts, ch 2 (*counts as an hdc*), hdc in next 9 [10, 12, 14] sts, turn.

Row 3: Sl st in first 3 [3, 4, 4] sts, sc in next 2 sts, hdc in next 5 [6, 7, 9] sts. (*10 [11, 13, 15] sts*)

Fasten off.

NECK & SHOULDER SHAPING

Row 1 (RS): Hold with RS facing, sk next 13 sts for neck, join in next st, ch 2, hdc in next 14 [15, 17, 19] sts, turn. (*15 [16, 18, 20] sts*)

Row 2: Ch 2, hdc in next 10 [11, 13, 15] sts, turn.

Row 3: Ch 2, hdc in next 5 [6, 7, 9] sts, sc in next 2 sts. (*10 [11, 13, 15] sts*)

Fasten off.

FRONT

Work as for Back until piece measures 15½ [16½, 17½, 18] inches from beg, ending by working a WS row, turn.

SHOULDER SHAPING

Row 1 (RS): Ch 2 (*counts as an hdc*), work 14 [15, 17, 19] sts, turn. (*15 [16, 18, 20] sts*)

Row 2: Sl st in first 2 sts, ch 2, hdc in each st across, turn. (*14 [15, 17, 19] sts*)

Row 3: Ch 2, hdc in each st to last hdc, turn, leaving rem st unworked. (*13 [15, 16, 18] sts*)

Row 4: Ch 2, dec, hdc in each st across, turn. (*12 [14, 15, 17] sts*)

For Small, Large & X-Large Sizes Only
Rows 5 & 6: Rep rows 3 and 4. (*10 [13, 15] sts*)

Work even until same length as Back to shoulder.

Fasten off.

For Medium Size Only
Rows 5 & 6: Rep rows 3 and 4.

Row 7: Rep row 3. (*11 sts*)

Work even until same length as Back to shoulder.

Fasten off.

NECK & SHOULDER SHAPING

Row 1 (RS): Hold with RS facing, sk next 13 sts, join in next st, ch 2, hdc in each rem st across, turn. (*15 [16, 18, 20] sts*)

Row 2: Ch 2, hdc in each st to last hdc, turn, leaving rem st unworked. (*14 [15, 17, 19] sts*)

Row 3: Ch 2, dec, hdc in each st across, turn. (*13 [15, 16, 18] sts*)

Row 4: Ch 2, hdc in each st to last hdc, turn, leaving rem st unworked. (*12 [14, 15, 17] sts*)

For Small, Large & X-Large Sizes Only
Rows 5 & 6: Rep rows 3 and 4. (*10 [13, 15] sts*)

Work even until same length as Back to shoulder.

Fasten off.

For Medium Size Only
Rows 5 & 6: Rep rows 3 and 4.

Row 7: Rep row 3. *(11 sts)*

Work even until same length as Back to shoulder.

Fasten off.

SLEEVES
Row 1: Ch 23 [23, 25, 27], hdc in 2nd ch from hook and each ch across, turn. *(21 [21, 23, 25] sts)*

Row 2: Ch 2 *(counts as an hdc)*, *ch 1, sk next hdc, hdc in next st; rep from * across, turn.

Row 3: Ch 2, hdc in each ch-1 sp and in each hdc across, turn.

Row 4: Ch 2, hdc in same st *(inc)*, hdc to last st, 2 hdc in last st *(inc)*, turn. *(23 [23, 25, 27] sts)*

Note: *Remainder of Sleeve is worked in hdc only.* Continuing in hdc, inc every 4th row 6 [3, 0, 0] times then every 3rd row 3 [7, 11, 11] times. *(41 [43, 47, 49] hdc)*

Work even until Sleeve measures 20½ [21, 21, 21½] inches from beg.

Fasten off.

ASSEMBLY
Sew shoulder seams.

NECK BAND
Rnd 1 (RS): Hold with RS facing, join with sc in one seam, sc evenly around, having a multiple of 6 sts; join with sl st in joining sc.

Rnd 2: Ch 2 *(counts as an hdc)*, hdc in next 3 sts, dec, *hdc in next 4 sts, dec; rep from * around, join with sl st in 2nd ch of beg ch-2.

Rnd 3: Ch 3 *(counts as an hdc and a ch-1 sp)*, *sk next st, hdc in next st, ch 1; rep from * around, join with sl st in 2nd ch of beg ch-3.

Rnd 4: Ch 2, hdc in each ch-1 sp and in each hdc around, join with sl st in 2nd ch of beg ch-2.

Fasten off.

FINISHING
Sew underarm and side seams. 🍀

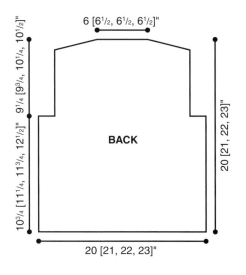

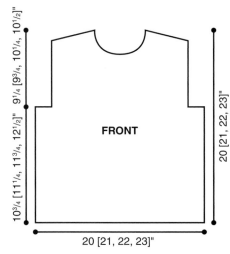

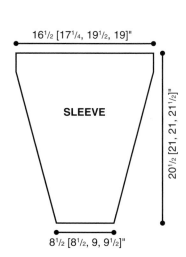

Festive-Style Cropped Cover-Ups

DESIGN BY EDIE ECKMAN

Child's Cover-Up

SKILL LEVEL EASY

FINISHED SIZES
Instructions given fit child's size 4; changes for sizes 6–8, 10 and 12 are in [ ].

FINISHED GARMENT MEASUREMENTS
Chest: 26 [31, 33, 35] inches

MATERIALS
 Lion Brand Chenille Thick & Quick super bulky (super chunky) weight yarn (100 yds per ball):
2 (3, 4, 4) balls #113 scarlet *(A)*
Lion Brand Yarn Fun Fur bulky (chunky) weight eyelash yarn
(1¾ oz/60 yds/50g per ball): 1 ball #100 white *(B)*
Size N/13/9mm crochet hook
Size P/15mm crochet hook or size needed to obtain gauge
Yarn needle

GAUGE
With larger hook and A: 6 sts = 4 inches;
8 rows = 4 inches
Take time to check gauge.

PATTERN NOTE
B is used doubled throughout.

Instructions

BACK
Row 1 (RS): With larger hook and A, ch 21 [25, 25, 27], sc in 2nd ch from hook and each ch across, turn. *(20 [24, 24, 26] sc)*

Row 2: Ch 1, sc in each sc across, turn.

Rep row 2 until piece measures 2 [3, 3, 3] inches, ending with a WS row.

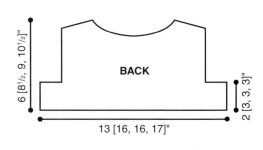

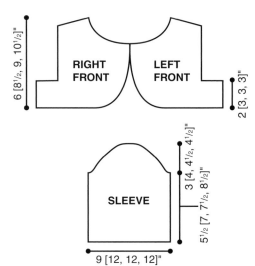

ARMHOLE SHAPING

Note: For **sc dec,** draw up lp in each of next 2 sts indicated, yo and draw through all 3 lps on hook.

Row 1 (RS): Sl st in first st, sc in next 18 [22, 22, 24] sts, turn, leaving rem st unworked.

Row 2: Ch 1, **sc dec** (see Note) in first 2 sc, sc in next 14 [18, 18, 20] sc, dec over last 2 sc, turn. (16 [20, 20, 22] sts)

For Sizes 4 & 10 Only
Row 3: Ch 1, sc in each sc, turn.

Rep row 3 until piece measures 5 [8] inches, ending with a WS row.

For Size 6–8 Only
Row 3: Ch 1, sc in each sc across, turn.

Row 4: Rep row 3.

Row 5: Ch 1, sc dec in first 2 sc, sc to last 2 sc, sc dec in last 2 sc, turn. (18 sts)

Rep row 3 until piece measures 7½ inches, ending with a WS row.

For Size 12 Only
Row 3: Ch 1, sc in each sc across, turn.

Rows 4–6: Rep row 3.

Row 7: Ch 1, sc dec in first 2 sc, sc to last 2 sc, sc dec over last 2 sc, turn. (20 sts)

Work even until piece measures 9½ inches, ending with a WS row.

RIGHT SHOULDER SHAPING
Row 1 (RS): Ch 1, sc in first 6 [7, 7, 7] sc, turn.

Row 2: Sl st in first 2 sts, sc in next 4 [5, 5, 5] sts, turn.

Row 3: Ch 1, sc in first 2 [3, 3, 3] sts, sc dec.

Fasten off.

LEFT SHOULDER SHAPING
Row 1 (RS): Hold with RS facing, sk next 4 [4, 6, 6] sts from Right Shoulder, attach yarn in next st, ch 1, sc in next 6 [7, 7, 7] sts, turn.

Row 2: Ch 1, sc in next 4 [5, 5, 5] sts, turn.

Row 3: Ch 1, sc dec, sc in next 2 [3, 3, 3] sts.

Fasten off.

LEFT FRONT
Row 1 (RS): With P hook and A, ch 9 [11, 11, 11], sc in 2nd ch from hook and in each ch across, turn. (8, [10, 10, 10] sts)

Note: Mark row 1 as RS.

Row 2: Ch 1, 2 sc in first st, sc in each sc across, turn. (9, [11, 11, 11] 1 sts)

For Sizes 4, 6–8 & 10 Only
Row 3: Ch 1, sc in each sc across, turn.

Rep row 3 until piece measures same as Back to armhole, ending with a WS row.

For Size 12 Only
Row 3: Ch 1, sc in each sc to last sc, 2 sc in last sc, turn. (12 sts)

Row 4: Ch 1, sc in each sc, turn.

Rep row 4 until piece measures same as back to armhole, ending with a WS row.

ARMHOLE SHAPING
Row 1 (RS): Sl st in first sc, sc in each sc across, turn.

Row 2: Ch 1, sc in first 6 [8, 8, 9] sc, dec, turn. (7 [9, 9, 10] sts)

For Size 4 Only
Row 3: Ch 1, sc in each sc across, turn.

Row 4: Rep row 3.

For Size 6–8 & 12 Only
Row 3: Ch 1, sc in each sc across, turn.

Row 4: Rep row 3.

Row 5: Ch 1, sc dec, sc in each sc across, turn. (8 [9] sts)

Row 6: Rep row 3.

For Size 10 Only
Row 3: Ch 1, sc in each sc across, turn.

Rows 4–6: Rep row 3.

NECK SHAPING

Row 1 (RS): Ch 1, sc in first 5 [7, 7, 7] sts, turn, leaving rem sts unworked.

Row 2: Ch 1, sc in each sc across, turn.

For Size 4 Only

Row 3: Ch 1, sc in each sc to last 2 sc, sc dec, turn. *(4 sts)*

Row 4: Ch 1, sc in each sc across, turn.

Row 5: Rep row 3.

Rep row 4 until piece measures same as Back.

Fasten off.

For Size 6–8 Only

Row 3: Ch 1, sc in each sc to last 2 sc, sc dec. turn. *(6 sts)*

Row 4: Ch 1, sc dec, sc in each sc across, turn. *(5 sts)*

Row 5: Rep row 3. *(4 sts)*

Row 6: Ch 1, sc in each sc across, turn.

Rep row 6 until piece measures same as Back.

Fasten off.

For Sizes 10 & 12 Only

Row 3: Ch 1, sc in each sc to last 2 sc, sc dec, turn. *(6 sts)*

Row 4: Ch 1, sc in each sc across, turn.

Rows 5–7: [Rep rows 3 and 4] twice. *(4 sts)*

Rep row 4 until piece measures same as Back.

Fasten off.

RIGHT FRONT

Row 1 (RS): With P hook and A, ch 9, [11, 11, 11], sc in 2nd ch from hook and each ch across, turn. *(8, [10, 10, 10] sts)*

Note: *Mark row 1 as RS.*

Row 2: Ch 1, sc in each st to last st, 2 sc in last st, turn. *(9, [11, 11, 11]1 sts)*

For Sizes 4, 6–8 & 10 Only
Row 3: Ch 1, sc in each sc across, turn.

Rep row 3 until piece measures same as Back to armhole, ending with a RS row.

For Size 12 Only
Row 3: Ch 1, turn, 2 sc in first sc, sc in each sc across, turn. *(12 sts)*

Row 4: Ch 1, sc in each sc across, turn.

Rep row 4 until piece measures same as Back to armhole, ending with a RS row.

ARMHOLE SHAPING
Row 1 (WS): Sl st in first sc, sc in each sc across, turn.

Row 2 (RS): Ch 1, sc in first 6 [8, 8, 9] sc, sc dec, turn. *(7 [9, 9, 10] sts)*

For Size 4 Only 1
Row 3: Ch 1, sc in each sc across, turn.

Row 4: Rep row 3.

For Size 6–8 & 12 Only
Row 3: Ch 1, sc in each sc across, turn.

Row 4: Rep row 3.

Row 5: Ch 1, sc dec, sc in each sc across, turn. *(8 [9] sts)*

Row 6: Rep row 3.

For Size 10 Only
Row 3: Ch 1, sc in each sc across, turn.

Rows 4–6: Rep row 3.

NECK SHAPING
Row 1 (WS): Ch 1, sc in first 5 [7, 7, 7] sts, turn, leaving rem sts unworked.

Row 2 (RS): Ch 1, sc in each sc across, turn.

For Size 4 Only
Row 3: Ch 1, sc in each sc to last 2 sc, sc dec, turn.

Row 4: Ch 1, sc in each sc across, turn.

Row 5: Rep row 3.

Rep row 4 until piece measures same as Back.

Fasten off.

For Size 6–8 Only
Row 3: Ch 1, sc in each sc to last 2 sc, sc dec. turn. *(6 sts)*

Row 4: Ch 1, sc dec, sc in each sc across, turn. *(5 sts)*

Row 5: Rep row 3. *(4 sts)*

Row 6: Ch 1, sc in each sc across, turn.

Rep row 6 until piece measures same as Back.

Fasten off.

For Sizes 10 & 12 Only
Row 3: Ch 1, sc in each sc to last 2 sc, sc dec, turn. *(6 sts)*

Row 4: Ch 1, sc in each sc across, turn.

Rows 5–7: [Rep rows 3 and 4] twice. *(4 sts)*

Rep row 4 until piece measures same as Back.

Fasten off.

SLEEVES
Row 1 (RS): With P hook and A, ch 15 [19, 19, 19], sc in 2nd ch from hook and each ch across, changing to B in last st, turn. *(14 [18, 18, 18] sts)*

Row 2: Ch 1, turn, sc across, changing to A in last sc, turn. Fasten off B.

Row 3: Ch 1, sc in each sc across, turn.

Rep row 3 until Sleeve measures 5½ [7, 7½, 8½] inches.

CAP SHAPING
Row 1 (RS): Sl st in first 2 sts, sc in next 10 [14, 14, 14] sts, turn, leaving rem sts unworked.

Row 2: Ch 1, sc dec, sc in next 6 [10, 10, 10] sts, dec, turn. (*8, [12, 12, 12] sts*)

For Size 4 Only
Row 3: Ch 1, sc in each sc across, turn.

Rows 4 & 5: Rep row 3.

Row 6: Ch 1, dec, sc to last 2 sts, dec, turn. (*6 sts*)

Rep row 3 until Sleeve measures 8½ inches.

Fasten off.

For Sizes 6–8, 10 & 12 Only
Row 3: Ch 1, sc in each sc across, turn.

Row 4: Ch 1, sc dec, sc in each sc to last 2 st, dec, turn. (*10 sts*)

Rows 5–8: [Rep rows 3 and 4] twice. (*6 sts*)

Rep row 3 until Sleeve measures 11 [12, 13] inches.

Fasten off.

ASSEMBLY
Sew shoulder and side seams.

EDGING
Rnd 1: Join A at center back neck edge, ch 1, sc evenly around neck, front and lower edges, working 3 sc in each front neck corner st, changing to B in last st, join with sl st in first sc.

Rnd 2: Ch 1, sc around, inc along front curve and dec around neck as necessary to allow band to lie flat, changing to A in last st, join in first sc.

Rnd 3: Ch 1, sc in each sc around, inc and dec as necessary.

Fasten off.

FINISHING
Sew underarm and Sleeve seams.

Adult's Cover-Up

SKILL LEVEL ◼◼◻◻
EASY

FINISHED SIZES
Instructions given fit woman's small; changes for medium, large and X-large are in [ ].

FINISHED GARMENT MEASUREMENTS
Chest: 40 [44, 48, 51] inches

MATERIALS
 Lion Brand Chenille Thick & Quick super bulky (super chunky) weight yarn (100 yds per ball): 4 [5, 6, 6] balls #113 scarlet (*A*)
 Lion Brand Fun Fur bulky (chunky) weight eyelash yarn (1¾ oz/60 yds/50g per ball): 1 ball #100 white (*B*)
N/13/9mm crochet hook
Size P/15mm crochet hook or size needed to obtain gauge
Yarn needle

GAUGE
With larger hook: 6 sts = 4 inches; 8 rows = 4 inches

PATTERN NOTE
B is used double throughout.

BACK
Row 1 (RS): With P hook and A, ch 31 [35, 37, 39], sc in 2nd ch from hook and each ch across, turn. (*30, [34, 36, 38] sts*)

Row 2: Ch 1, sc in each sc across, turn.

Rep row 2 until piece measures 4 [5, 5, 5] inches from beg, ending with a WS row.

ARMHOLE SHAPING
Note: *For **sc dec**, draw up lp in each of next 2 sts indicated, yo and draw through all 3 lps on hook.*

Row 1 (RS): Sl st in first 2 [2, 3, 3] sts, sc in next 26 [30, 30, 32] sts, turn, leaving rem sts unworked.

For Small Size Only
Row 2: Ch 1, sc in each sc across, turn.

Row 3: Ch 1, **sc dec** *(see Note)*, sc in each sc to last 2 sc, sc dec, turn. *(24 sts)*

Rows 4–6: Rep row 2.

Row 7: Rep row 3. *(22 sts)*

Rep row 2 until piece measures 10 inches, ending by working a WS row.

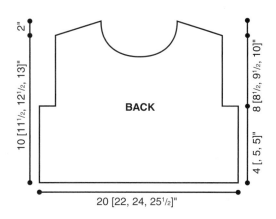

BACK

2"

10 [11½, 12½, 13]"

8 [8½, 9½, 10]"

4 [, 5, 5]"

20 [22, 24, 25½]"

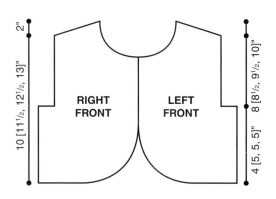

RIGHT FRONT **LEFT FRONT**

2"

10 [11½, 12½, 13]"

8 [8½, 9½, 10]"

4 [5, 5, 5]"

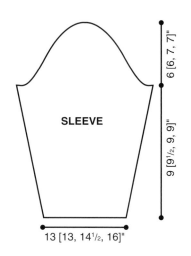

SLEEVE

6 [6, 7, 7]"

9 [9½, 9, 9]"

13 [13, 14½, 16]"

For Medium, Large & X-Large Sizes Only
Row 2: Ch 1, **sc dec** *(see Note)*, sc to last 2 sts, dec, turn. *(28, [28, 30] sts)*

Row 3: Rep row 2. *(26 [26, 28] sts)*

Row 4: Ch 1, sc in each sc across, turn.

Rows 5 & 6: Rep row 4.

Row 7: Rep row 2. *(24 [24, 26] sts)*

Rep row 4 until piece measures 11½ [12½, 13] inches, ending by working a WS row.

RIGHT NECK & SHOULDER SHAPING
Row 1 (RS): Ch 1, sc in next 8 [9, 8, 9] sts, turn.

Row 2: Sl st in first 2 [2, 1, 1] sts, sc in next 6 [7, 7, 8] sts, turn.

Row 3: Ch 1, sc in first 4 [5, 5, 7] sts, sc dec, turn.

Row 4: Ch 1, sc in first 3 sts, turn leaving rem sts unworked.

Fasten off.

LEFT NECK & SHOULDER SHAPING
Row 1 (RS): Hold with RS facing, sk next 6 [6, 8, 8] sts from Right Shoulder Shaping, attach yarn in next st, ch 1, sc in next 8 [9, 8, 9] sts, turn.

Row 2: Ch 1, sc in first 6 [7, 7, 8] sts, turn, leaving rem sts unworked.

Row 3: Ch 1, dec, sc in next 4 [5, 4, 6] sts, turn.

Row 4: Ch 1, sl st in first 2 [3, 3, 4] sts, sc in next 3 sts.

Fasten off.

LEFT FRONT
Row 1 (RS): With P hook and A, ch 13 [14, 16, 16], sc in 2nd ch from hook and each ch across, turn. *(12, [13, 15, 15] sts)*

Row 2: Ch 1, 2 sc in first st, sc in each sc across, turn. *(13, [14, 16, 16] sts)*

Row 3: Ch 1, sc in each sc to last sc, 2 sc in last sc, turn. *(14, [15, 17, 17] sts)*

For Small & Large Sizes Only
Row 4: Ch 1, sc in each sc across, turn. *(14 [17] sts)*

Rep row 4 until piece measures same as Back to armhole, ending with a WS row.

For Medium & X-Large Sizes Only
Row 4: Ch 1, 2 sc in first st, sc in each sc across, turn. (*16, [18] sts*)

Row 5: Ch 1, sc in each sc across, turn.

Rep row 5 until piece measures same as Back to armhole, ending with a WS row.

ARMHOLE SHAPING
Row 1 (RS): Sl st in first 2 [2, 3, 3] sts, sc in each st across, turn. (*12 [14, 14, 14] sts*)

For Small Size Only
Row 2: Ch 1, sc in each sc across, turn.

Row 3: Ch 1, dec, sc in each sc across, turn. (*11 sts*)

Rows 4–6: Rep row 2.

Row 7: Rep row 3. (*10 sts*)

Rep row 2 until piece measures 8½ inches, ending by working a WS row.

For Medium, Large & X-Large Sizes Only
Row 2: Ch 1, sc dec, sc to last 2 sts, turn. (*13 sts*)

Row 3: Rep row 2. (*12 sts*)

Row 4: Ch 1, sc in each sc across, turn.

Rows 5 & 6: Rep row 4.

Row 7: Rep row 2. (*11 sts*)

Rep row 4 until piece measures 9½ [9½, 10½] inches, ending with a RS row.

NECK & SHOULDER SHAPING
Row 1 (WS): Sl st in first 2 sts, sc in next 8 [9, 9, 9] sts, turn.

Row 2: Ch 1, sc in next 6 [7, 7, 7] sts, dec, turn.

Row 3: Ch 1, sc dec, sc in next 5 [6, 6, 6] sts, turn.

Row 4: Ch 1, sc in first 5 [6, 6, 6] sts, turn.

Rows 5 & 6: Ch 1, sc in each st, turn.

Row 7: Ch 1, sc in first 3 sts. Fasten off, leaving rem sts unworked.

RIGHT FRONT
Row 1 (RS): With P hook and A, ch 13 [14, 16, 16], sc in 2nd ch from hook and each ch across, turn. (*12, [13, 15, 15] sts*)

Row 2: Ch 1, sc to last st, 2 sc in last st, turn. (*13, [14, 16, 16] sts*)

Row 3: Ch 1, 2 sc in first sc, sc in each st across, turn. (*14, [15, 17, 17] sts*)

For Small & Large Sizes Only
Row 4: Ch 1, sc in each sc across, turn. (*14 [17] sts*)

Rep row 4 until piece measures same as Back to armhole, ending with a WS row.

For Medium & X-Large Sizes Only
Row 4: Ch 1, 2 sc in first st, sc in each sc across, turn. (*16, [18] sts*)

Row 5: Ch 1, sc in each sc across, turn.

Rep row 5 until piece measures same as Back to armhole, ending with a RS row.

ARMHOLE SHAPING
Row 1 (WS): Sl st in first 2 [2, 3, 3] sts, sc in each st across, turn. (*12 [14, 14, 14] sts*)

For Small Size Only
Row 2 (RS): Ch 1, sc in each sc across, turn.

Row 3: Ch 1, sc dec, sc in each sc across, turn. (*11 sts*)

Rows 4–6: Rep row 2.

Row 7: Rep row 3. (*10 sts*)

Rep row 2 until piece measures 8½ inches, ending by working a WS row.

For Medium, Large & X-Large Sizes Only
Row 2 (RS): Ch 1, sc dec, sc to last 2 sts, turn. (*13 sts*)

Row 3: Rep row 2. (*12 sts*)

Row 4: Ch 1, sc in each sc across, turn.

Rows 5 & 6: Rep row 4.

Row 7: Rep row 2. *(11 sts)*

Rep row 4 until piece measures 9½ [9½, 10½] inches, ending with a WS row.

NECK & SHOULDER SHAPING
Row 1 (RS): Sl st in first 2 sts, sc in next 8 [9, 9, 9] sts, turn.

Row 2: Ch 1, sc in next 6 [7, 7, 7] sts, sc dec, turn.

Row 3: Ch 1, sc dec, sc in next 5 [6, 6, 6] sts, turn.

Row 4: Ch 1, sc in first 5 [6, 6, 6] sts, turn.

Rows 5 & 6: Ch 1, sc in each st, turn.

Row 7: Ch 1, sc in first 3 sts. Fasten off, leaving rem sts unworked.

SLEEVES
Row 1 (RS): With P hook and A, ch 21 [21, 23, 25], sc in 2nd ch from hook and each ch across, changing to B in last st, turn. *(20, [20, 22, 24] sts)*

Row 2: Ch 1, sc in each st across, changing to A in last st, turn. Fasten off B.

Row 3: Ch 1, sc in each sc across, turn.

Rows 4–7: Rep row 3.

Row 8: Ch 1, 2 sc in next sc, sc in each sc to last sc, 2 sc in last sc, turn. *(22 [22, 24, 26] sts)*

For Small, Medium & Large Sizes Only
Work even until Sleeve measures 9 [9½, 9] inches.

For X-Large Size Only
Row 9: Ch 1, sc in each sc across, turn.

Rows 10–12: Rep row 8.

Row 13: Ch 1, 2 sc in next sc, sc in each sc to last sc, 2 sc in last sc, turn. *(28 sts)*

Rep row 9 until Sleeve measures 9 inches.

CAP SHAPING
Row 1: Sl st in first 2 sts, sc in next 18 [18, 20, 24] sts, turn, leaving rem sts unworked.

Row 2: Ch 1, sc dec, sc in next 14 [14, 16, 20] sts, dec, turn. *(16 [16, 18, 22] sts)*

For Small Size Only
Row 3: Ch 1, sc dec, sc in each sc to last 2 sc, dec, turn. *(14 sts)*

Row 4: Ch 1, sc in each sc across, turn.

Rows 5–12: Rep Rows 3 and 4. *(6 sts)*

For Medium, Large & X-Large Sizes Only
Row 3: Ch 1, sc in each sc across, turn.

Row 4: Ch 1, sc dec, sc in each sc to last 2 sc, dec, turn. *(14 [16, 20] sts)*

Rows 5–12 [14, 14]: Rep Rows 3 and 4. *(6 sts)*

Fasten off.

ASSEMBLY
Sew shoulder and side seams.

EDGING
Rnd 1: Join A at center back neck edge, ch 1, sc evenly around Neck, front and lower edges, working 3 sc in each Front Neck corner st, changing to B in last st, join with sl st in first sc.

Rnd 2: Ch 1, sc around, inc along front curve and dec around Neck as necessary to allow band to lie flat, changing to A in last st, join in first sc.

Rnd 3: Ch 1, sc in each sc around, inc and dec as necessary.

Fasten off.

FINISHING
Sew underarm and Sleeve seams.

Soft & Sophisticated Short Bolero

DESIGN BY ZELDA WORKMAN

SKILL LEVEL

FINISHED SIZES
Instructions given fit woman's small; changes for medium, large, X-large and 2X-large are in [ ].

FINISHED GARMENT MEASUREMENTS
Chest: 32 [37, 42] inches
Length: 16 inches

MATERIALS
 Lion Brand Fancy Fur bulky (chunky) weight eyelash yarn
(1¾ oz/39 yds/50g per ball): 5 [6, 7] balls #257 stormy sea
Size N/13/9mm crochet hook or size needed to obtain gauge
Yarn needle

GAUGE
10¼ sts = 4 inches; 8 rows = 4 inches
Take time to check gauge.

PATTERN NOTES
The texture of this yarn makes it difficult to count stitches and rows after they are made, so count carefully as you work. It is helpful to write down each row number as it is finished.

When making slip stitches on shaping rows, make sure to slip stitch into the chains and not into the chain spaces.

Instructions

BACK
Row 1 (WS): Ch 42 [48, 54], sc in 2nd ch from hook and in each ch across, turn. (*41 [47, 53] sc*)

Row 2 (RS): Ch 1, sc in first sc, *ch 1, sk next sc, sc in next sc; rep from * across, turn. (*21 [24, 27] sc and 20 [23, 26] ch-1 sps*)

Row 3: Ch 1, sc in first sc, *ch 1, sk next ch, sc in next sc; rep from * across, turn.

Rows 4–16: Rep row 3.

ARMHOLE SHAPING
Row 1: Sl st in first 4 sts, ch 1, sc in next sc, *ch 1, sk next ch, sc in next sc, rep from * to last 4 sts, turn, leaving rem sts unworked. (*17 [20, 23] sc and 16 [19, 22] ch-1 sps*)

Row 2: Ch 1, sc in first sc, *ch 1, sk next ch, sc in next sc; rep from * across, turn.

Rows 3–15: Rep row 2.

Row 16: Work in established pat across 11 [13, 17] sts, sl st in next 11 [13, 11] sts, work in established pat across rem 11 [13, 17] sts.

Fasten off.

RIGHT FRONT
Row 1 (WS): Ch 15 [19, 23], sc in 2nd ch from hook and in each ch to last ch, 2 sc in last ch, turn. (*15, [19, 23] sc*)

Row 2 (RS): Ch 1, (sc, ch 1, sc) in first sc, *ch 1, sk next sc, sc in next sc; rep from * across, turn. (*9 [11, 13] sc and 8 [10, 12] ch-1 sps*)

Row 3: Ch 1, sc in first sc, *ch 1, sk next ch, sc in next sc; rep from * across, ch 1, sc in same st as last sc, turn. (*10 [12, 14] sc and 9 [11, 13] ch-1 sps*)

4 [5, 6]"

8"

8"

BACK

16 [18½, 21]"

4 [5, 6]"

8"

8"

RIGHT FRONT

LEFT FRONT

8 [9¾, 11]"

Row 4: Ch 1, (sc, ch 1, sc) in first sc, *ch 1, sk next ch, sc in next sc; rep from * across, turn. *(11 [13, 15] sc and 10 [12, 14] ch-1 sps)*

Row 5: Ch 1, sc in first sc, *ch 1, sk next ch, sc in next sc; rep from * across, turn.

Rows 6–16: Rep row 5.

ARMHOLE SHAPING
Row 1: Sl st in first 4 sts, ch 1, sc in next sc, *ch 1, sk next ch, sc in next sc, rep from * across, turn. *(9 [11, 13] sc and 8 [10, 12] ch-1 sps)*

Row 2: Ch 1, sc in first sc, *ch 1, sk next ch, sc in next sc; rep from * across, turn.

Rows 3–11: Rep row 2.

NECK SHAPING
Row 1: Sl st in first 4 sts, ch 1, sc in next sc, *ch 1, sk next ch, sc in next sc, rep from * across, turn. *(7 [9, 11] sc and 6 [8, 10] ch-1 sps)*

Row 2: Ch 1, sc in first sc, *ch 1, sk next sc, sc in next sc, rep from * to last 2 sts, turn, leaving rem sts unworked. *(6 [8, 10] sc and 5 [7, 9] ch-1 sps)*

Row 3: Ch 1, sc in first sc, *ch 1, sk next ch, sc in next sc; rep from * across, turn.

Rows 4 & 5: Rep row 3.

Fasten off.

LEFT FRONT
Row 1 (WS): Ch 15 [19, 23], 2 sc in 2nd ch from hook, sc in each ch across, turn. *(15 [19, 13] sc)*

Row 2 (RS): Ch 1, sc in first sc, *ch 1, sk next sc, sc in next sc; rep from * across, ch 1, sc in same st as last sc, turn. *(9 [11, 13] sc and 8 [10, 12] ch-1 sps)*

Row 3: Ch 1, (sc, ch 1, sc) in first sc, *ch 1, sk next ch, sc in next sc, rep from * across, turn. *(10 [12, 14] sc and 9 [11, 13] ch-1 sps)*

Row 4: Ch 1, sc in first sc, *ch 1, sk next ch, sc in next sc; rep from * across, ch 1, sc in same st as last sc, turn. *(11 [13, 15] sc and 10 [12, 14] ch-1 sps)*

Row 5: Ch 1, sc in first sc, *ch 1, sk next ch, sc in next sc; rep from * across, turn.

Rows 6–16: Rep row 5.

ARMHOLE SHAPING
Row 1: Ch 1, sc in first sc, *ch 1, sk next ch, sc in next sc; rep from * to last 4 sts, turn, leaving rem sts unworked. *(9 [11, 13] sc and 8 [10, 12] ch-1 sps)*

Row 2: Ch 1, sc in first sc, *ch 1, sk next ch, sc in next sc; rep from * across, turn.

Rows 3–11: Rep row 2.

NECK SHAPING
Row 1: Ch 1, sc in first sc, *ch 1, sk next ch, sc in next sc, rep from * to last 4 sts, turn. *(7 [9, 11] sc and 6 [8, 10] ch-1 sps)*

Row 2: Sl st in first 2 sts, ch 1, sc in next sc, *ch 1, sk next ch, sc in next sc, rep from * across, turn. *(6 [8, 10] sc and 5 [7, 9] ch-1 sps)*

Row 3: Ch 1, sc in first sc, *ch 1, sk next ch, sc in next sc; rep from * across, turn.

Rows 4 & 5: Rep row 3.

Fasten off and weave in all ends.

FINISHING
Sew Front to Back at shoulders and side seams.

Scrumptious-to-the-Touch Vest

DESIGN BY NAZANIN FARD

SKILL LEVEL
INTERMEDIATE

FINISHED SIZES
Instructions given fit woman's small; changes for medium and large are in [ ].

FINISHED GARMENT MEASUREMENTS
Chest: 33 [37½, 42] inches

MATERIALS
Patons Twister bulky (chunky) weight yarn (1¾ oz/47 yds/50g per ball):
10 [13, 16] balls #05711 fruit loops
Size K/10½/6.5mm crochet hook or size needed to obtain gauge
Yarn needle

GAUGE
12 sts = 4 inches

PATTERN NOTE
Vest is worked in one piece to armhole.

Instructions

BODY
Note: For **dc dec,** *[yo, draw up lp in next st, yo, draw through 2 lps on hook] twice, yo and draw through all 3 lps on hook.*

Row 1: Starting at bottom edge, ch 83 [95, 107], dc in 3rd ch from hook and in each ch across, turn. *(81 [93, 105] dc)*

Row 2: Ch 2, dc in each dc across, turn.

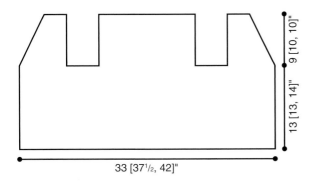

33 [37½, 42]"

13 [13, 14]"

9 [10, 10]"

Rep row 2 until piece measures 15 [15, 16] inches, ending by working a RS row.

Next row: Ch 2, **dc dec** *(see Note)*, dc in each st to last 2 sts, dc dec, turn. *(79, [91,103] sts)*

RIGHT FRONT
Row 1 (RS): Ch 2, dc in next 14 [18, 20] sts, turn, leaving rem sts unworked.

Row 2: Ch 2, dc in each dc to last 2 dc, dc dec over last 2 dc, turn. *(13 [17, 19] sts)*

Rows 3–8: Rep rows 1 and 2. *(10 [14, 16] sts)*

Row 9: Ch 3 *(counts as a dc)*, dc in each dc across, turn.

Rep row 9 until piece measures 9 [10, 10] inches along armhole edge.

Fasten off.

LEFT FRONT
Row 1 (RS): Hold with RS facing, sk next 41 [44, 50] sts from Right Front, attach yarn in next st, ch 3 *(counts as a dc)*, dc in next 13 [17, 19] sts, turn, leaving rem st unworked. *(14 [18, 20] sts)*

Row 2: Ch 2, dc dec, dc in each st across, turn.

Row 3: Ch 3, dc in each dc to last 2 dc, dc dec, turn.

Rows 4–7: Rep rows 2 and 3.

Row 8: Rep row 2. *(10 [14, 16] sts)*

Row 9: Ch 3, dc in each dc across, turn.

Rep row 9 until piece measures 9 [10, 10] inches along armhole edge.

Fasten off.

BACK
Row 1 (RS): Hold piece with RS facing, sk next 10, [11, 13] sts from the Right Front, attach yarn in next st, ch 3, dc in next 30 [33, 37] sts, turn, leaving rem 10 [11, 13] unworked sts for the left armhole.

Row 2: Ch 3, dc in each dc across, turn.

Rep row 2 until Back measures 25 [25, 26] inches from lower edge.

Fasten off.

FINISHING
Sew the Right and Left Front shoulder to Back matching sts. ❧

Green With Envy Sweater Jacket

DESIGN BY DARLA SIMS

SKILL LEVEL
EASY

FINISHED SIZES
Instructions given fit woman's small; changes for medium, large, X-large and 2X-large are in [ ].

FINISHED GARMENT MEASUREMENTS
Chest: 40 [44, 48, 52, 56] inches

MATERIALS
Moda Dea Vixen bulky (chunky) weight yarn (1¾ oz/89 yds/50g per ball):

10 [11, 12, 13, 14] balls #3682 green with envy Size H/8/5mm and J/10/6mm crochet hooks or sizes needed to obtain gauge
Yarn needle
⅝-inch buttons: 7
Yarn needle
Stitch markers

GAUGE
5 sc = 2 inches
Take time to check gauge

Instructions

BACK
Row 1 (RS): Using larger hook, ch 51 [57, 61, 67, 71], hdc in 3rd ch from hook and in each ch across, turn. *(50 [56, 60, 66, 70] hdc)*

Rows 2 & 3: Ch 2 *(counts as a hdc)*, hdc in each hdc across, turn.

SIDE SHAPING
Note: *For* ***hdc dec****, yo, pull up lp in st indicated, yo, pull up lp in next st, yo and draw through all 5 lps on hook.*

Row 4: Ch 2, **hdc dec** *(see Note)* in next 2 sts, hdc in each hdc to last 2 sts, hdc dec in last 2 sts, turn. *(48 [54, 58, 64, 68] hdc)*

Row 5: Ch 2, hdc in each st across, turn.

Rows 6–9: [Rep rows 1 and 2] twice. *(44 [50, 54, 60, 64] hdc)*

Rows 10–13: Rep row 5.

Row 14: Ch 2, hdc in first st *(inc)*, hdc to last st, 2 hdc in last st *(inc)*, turn. *(46 [52, 56, 62, 66] hdc)*

Row 15: Rep row 5.

Rows 16–19: [Rep rows 12 and 13] twice. *(50 [56, 60, 66, 70] hdc)*

Work even until Back measures 13 inches.

Fasten off.

ARMHOLE SHAPING
Row 1: With RS facing, sk first 6 [7, 9, 10, 10] sts. Attach yarn in next st, ch 2 *(counts as a hdc)*, hdc in next 37 [41, 41, 45, 49] hdc, turn, leaving rem sts unworked.

Row 2: Ch 2, hdc in each hdc, turn.

Rep row 2 until armhole measures 9 [9½, 10, 10½, 11] inches.

Fasten off.

RIGHT FRONT
Row 1 (RS): Ch 26 [29, 31, 34, 36], hdc in 3rd ch from hook and in each ch across, turn. *(25 [28, 30, 33, 35 hdc)*

Row 2: Ch 2, hdc in each hdc across, turn.

Row 3: Rep row 2.

Row 4: Ch 2, hdc dec, hdc in each hdc across, turn. *(24 [27, 29, 32, 34] hdc)*

Rows 5–8: [Rep rows 3 and 4] twice. *(22 [25, 27, 30, 32] hdc)*

Rows 9–13: Rep row 2.

Row 14: Ch 2, hdc in first st (*inc*), hdc in each hdc across, turn. (*23 [26, 28, 31, 33] hdc*)

Row 15: Rep row 2.

Rows 16–19: [Rep rows 14 and 15] twice. (*25 [28, 30, 33, 35] hdc*)

Rep row 2 until piece measures same as Back to armhole, ending with a RS row.

Fasten off.

ARMHOLE SHAPING
Row 1: With WS facing, sk first 6 [7, 9, 10, 10) hdc, attach yarn in next hdc, ch 2 (*counts as a hdc*), hdc in each hdc across, turn. (*19 [21, 21, 23, 25] hdc*)

Row 2: Ch 2, hdc in each hdc across, turn.

Rep row 2 until piece measures 3 [3, 3½, 3½, 3½) inches less than back, ending with a WS row.

NECK SHAPING
Row 1: With RS facing, sk first 5 [5, 6, 6, 7] sts, hdc in each hdc across, turn. (*14 [16, 15, 17, 18] hdc*)

Row 2: Ch 2, hdc in each hdc across, turn.

Row 3: Ch 2, hdc dec, hdc in each st across, turn. (*13 [15, 14, 16, 17] hdc*)

Rows 4–7: [Rep rows 2 and 3] twice. (*11 [13, 12, 14, 15] hdc*)

Rep row 2 until armhole measures same as Back.

Fasten off.

LEFT FRONT
Row 1 (RS): Ch 26 [29, 31, 34, 36], hdc in 3rd ch from hook and in each ch across, turn. (*25 [28, 30, 33, 35] hdc*)

Row 2: Ch 2, hdc in each hdc across, turn.

Row 3: Rep row 2.

Row 4: Ch 2, hdc to last 2 sts, hdc dec, turn. (*24 [27, 29, 32, 34] hdc*)

Rows 5–8: [Rep rows 3 and 4] twice. (*22 [25, 27, 30, 32] hdc*)

Rows 9–13: Rep row 2.

Row 14: Ch 2, hdc to last st, 2 hdc in last st (*inc*), turn. (*23 [26, 28, 31, 33] hdc*)

Row 15: Rep row 2.

Rows 16–19: [Rep rows 14 and 15] twice. (*25 [28, 30, 33, 35] hdc*)

Rep row 2 until front measures same as Back to armhole, ending with a RS row.

Fasten off.

ARMHOLE SHAPING
Row 1: Ch 2, hdc to last 6 [7, 9, 10, 10] hdc, turn, leaving rem sts unworked. (*19 [21, 21, 23, 25] hdc*)

Row 2: Ch 2, hdc in each hdc across, turn.

Rep row 2 until piece measures 3 [3, 3½, 3½, 3½] inches less than Back, ending with a WS row.

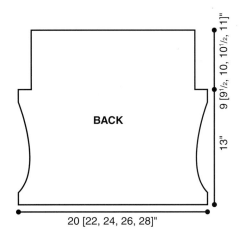

BACK

9 [9½, 10, 10½, 11]"

13"

20 [22, 24, 26, 28]"

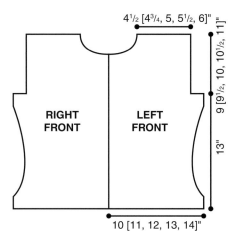

4½ [4¾, 5, 5½, 6]"

RIGHT FRONT

LEFT FRONT

9 [9½, 10, 10½, 11]"

13"

10 [11, 12, 13, 14]"

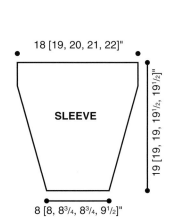

18 [19, 20, 21, 22]"

SLEEVE

19 [19, 19, 19½, 19½]"

8 [8, 8¾, 8¾, 9½]"

NECK SHAPING

Row 1: Ch 2, hdc to last 5 [5, 6, 6, 7] hdc, turn, leaving rem sts unworked. *(14 [16, 15, 17, 18] hdc)*

Row 2: Ch 2, hdc in each hdc across, turn.

Row 3: Ch 2, hdc to last 2 sts, hdc dec, turn. *(13, 15, 14, 16, 17 hdc)*

Rows 4–7: [Rep rows 2 and 3] twice. *(11, 13, 12, 14, 15 hdc)*

Rep row 2 until armhole measures same as Back.

Fasten off.

SLEEVES

Row 1: Ch 21 [21, 23, 23, 25], hdc in 3rd ch from hook and in each ch across, turn. *(20 [20, 22, 22, 24] hdc)*

Row 2: Ch 2, hdc in each hdc across, turn.

Row 3: Ch 2, 2 hdc in next st *(inc)*, hdc to last st, 2 hdc in last st *(inc)*, turn. *(22 [22, 24, 24, 26] hdc)*

Rows 4–27 [29, 31, 33, 37]: Rep rows 2 and 3. *(46 [48, 50, 52, 56] hdc)*

Rep row 2 until Sleeve measures 19 [19, 19½, 19½, 19½] inches.

Fasten off.

FINISHING

Sew Fronts to Back. Matching center of Sleeves to shoulder seams, sew in Sleeves. Sew Sleeve and side in 1 continuous seam.

EDGING
SLEEVE EDGING

Using smaller hook, attach yarn at seam and work sc evenly around Sleeve edge, join with sl st in first sc.

Fasten off.

FRONT, NECK & BOTTOM EDGING

Using smaller hook, attach yarn at seam, sc evenly around, working 3 sc in each corner, join.

Fasten off.

BUTTON LOOPS

Place markers for 7 buttons on Left Front, spacing evenly. Using smaller hook, attach yarn to Right Front in st that corresponds with lowest marker; *ch 4, sl st in same st, sk next st, sl st in next st; rep from * 6 times more.

Fasten off.

SCALLOP EDGING

Using smaller hook, attach yarn with sl st to front bottom corner of Left Side, *ch 6, sl st in same st, sk next st, sl st in next st; rep from * across.

Fasten off.

FINISHING

Sew on buttons opposite button lps. 🎔

Cool Weather Posh Jacket

DESIGN BY DARLA SIMS

SKILL LEVEL
EASY

FINISHED SIZES
Instructions given fit woman's small; changes for medium, large, X-large and 2X-large are in [ ].

FINISHED GARMENT MEASUREMENTS
Chest: 40 [44, 48, 52, 56] inches

MATERIALS
 Patons Bohemian super bulky (super chunky) weight yarn (2⅖ oz/68 yds/80g per ball): 10 [11, 12, 13, 14] balls #11520 copper chaos *(A)*
 Patons Allure super bulky (super chunky) weight yarn (1¾ oz/47 yds/50g per ball): 2 balls #04013 mink *(B)*
Size K/10½/6.5mm crochet hook or size needed to obtain gauge
Yarn needle
1 yd leather lace
Yarn needle
2 wooden beads

GAUGE
8 hdc = 4 inches; 7 rows = 4 inches
Take time to check gauge.

Instructions

BACK
Row 1 (RS): Using A, ch 41 [45, 49, 53, 57], hdc in 3rd ch from hook and in each ch across, turn. *(40 [44, 48, 52, 56] hdc)*

Row 2: Ch 2 *(counts as a hdc)*, hdc in each hdc across, turn.

Rep row 2 until piece measures 23 [23½, 24, 24½, 25] inches.

Fasten off.

RIGHT FRONT
Row 1 (RS): Using A, ch 21 [23, 25, 27, 29], hdc in 3rd ch from hook and in each ch across, turn. *(20 [2, 24, 26, 28] hdc)*

Row 2: Ch 2, hdc in each hdc across, turn.

Rep row 2 until piece measures 12 inches, ending with a RS row.

V-NECK SHAPING
Note: *For **hdc dec,** yo, pull up lp in st indicated, yo, pull up lp in next st, yo and draw through all 5 lps on hook.*

Row 1: Ch 2, hdc to last 2 hdc, **hdc dec** *(see Note)* in last 2 hdc, turn. *(19 [21, 23, 25, 27] hdc)* Mark last st.

Row 2: Ch 2, hdc in each hdc across, turn.

Row 3: Ch 2, hdc to last 2 hdc, hdc dec, turn. *(18 [20, 22, 24, 26] hdc)*

Row 4: Ch 2, hdc in each hdc across, turn.

Rows 5–16 [16, 16, 18, 18]: Rep rows 3 and 4. *(12 [14, 16, 17, 19] hdc)*

Rep row 4 until piece measures same as back.

Fasten off.

LEFT FRONT
Row 1: Using A, ch 21 [23, 25, 27, 29], hdc in 3rd ch from hook and in each ch across, turn. *(20 [22, 24, 26, 28] hdc)*

Row 2: Ch 2, hdc in each hdc across, turn.

Rep row 2 until piece measures 12 inches, ending with a RS row.

V-NECK SHAPING
Note: *For **beg hdc dec,** yo, pull up lp in st indicated, pull up lp in next st, yo and draw through all 4 lps on hook.*

Row 1: Ch 1, **beg hdc dec** *(see Note)* in first 2 hdc, hdc in each hdc across, turn. *(19 [21, 23, 25, 27] hdc)*

Mark first st.

Row 2: Ch 2, hdc in each hdc across, turn.

Row 3: Ch 1, beg hdc dec in first 2 hdc, hdc in each hdc across, turn. *(18 [20, 22, 24, 26] hdc)*

Row 4: Ch 2, hdc in each hdc across, turn.

Rows 5–16 [16, 16, 18, 18]: Rep rows 3 and 4. *(12 [14, 16, 17, 19] hdc)*

Rep row 4 until piece measures same as Back.

Fasten off.

SLEEVES

Row 1: Using A, ch 21 [23, 25, 25, 27], hdc in 3rd ch from hook and in each ch across, turn. *(20 [22, 24, 24, 26] hdc)*

Row 2: Ch 2, hdc in first st *(inc)*, hdc to last st, 2 hdc in last st *(inc)*, turn. *(22 [24, 26, 26, 28] hdc)*

Row 3: Ch 2, hdc in each ch across, turn.

Row 4: Ch 2, hdc in first st *(inc)*, hdc to last st, 2 hdc in last st *(inc)*, turn. *(24 [26, 28, 28, 30] hdc)*

Rows 5–16 [16, 16, 18, 18]: Rep rows 3 and 4. *(36 [38, 40, 42, 44] hdc)*

Rep row 4 until Sleeve measures 18 [18, 18, 18½, 18½] inches.

Fasten off.

ASSEMBLY

Sew shoulders. Place markers 9 [9½, 10, 10½, 11] inches on either side of shoulder seam for armhole. Fold sleeve in half, matching center of Sleeve to seam, sew Sleeve in between markers. Sew Sleeve and side in 1 continuous seam.

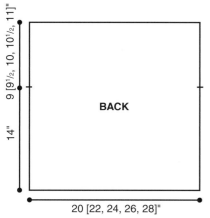

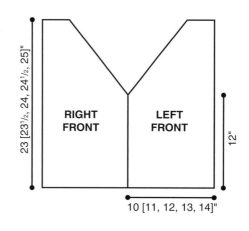

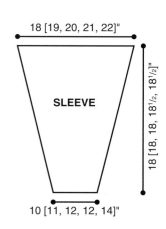

SLEEVE EDGING

Rnd 1 (RS): Attach B in seam of 1 Sleeve, work 19 sc evenly around Sleeve; join in first sc.

Rnds 2–4: Ch 2 (*counts as a hdc*), hdc in each sc; join in 2nd ch of beg ch-2.

Fasten off.

Rep for other Sleeve.

COLLAR

Row 1 (RS): With RS facing, attach B to marked st on Right Front, ch 1, sc in same st, work 25 [26, 27, 30, 32] sc to shoulder seam, work 16 [16, 16, 18, 18] sc across back neck, work 26 [27, 28, 29, 31] sc from shoulder seam to marked st on Left Front, turn. (*68 [70, 72, 76, 80] sc*)

Row 2: Ch 2, hdc in first st (*inc*), hdc in each st to shoulder seam, hdc dec, hdc in each st across back neck to shoulder seam, hdc dec, hdc to last st, 2 hdc in last st (*inc*), turn.

Row 3: Ch 2, hdc in first st (*inc*), hdc in each st to last st, 2 hdc in last st (*inc*), turn. (*70 [72, 74, 78, 82] hdc*)

Rows 4–7: Rep row 3. (*78 [80, 82, 86, 90] hdc*)

Fasten off.

FINISHING

Cut leather lace in half. Thread one bead on each piece of lace and knot above and below each bead. Tie and knot lace to front edge. 🍂

Spirited Fur-Trimmed Sweater Jacket

DESIGN BY TAMMY C. HILDEBRAND

SKILL LEVEL ■■□□
EASY

FINISHED SIZES
Instructions given fit woman's X-small; changes for small, medium, large and X-large are in [ ].

FINISHED GARMENT MEASUREMENTS
Chest: 9 [33, 37, 41, 45] inches

MATERIALS

Moda Dea Ticker Tape bulky (chunky) weight tape yarn (1¾ oz/67 yds/50g per ball):
10 [12, 15, 17, 20] balls #9507 festival *(A)*

Moda Dea Zing light (light worsted) weight yarn (1¾ oz/87 yds/50g per ball):
2 [3, 4, 6, 7] balls #1191 grape frost *(B)*
Size K/10½/6.5mm crochet hook or size needed to obtain gauge
Yarn needle
1 frog closure
Sewing needle and matching thread

GAUGE
12 sc = 4 inches; 15 sc rows = 4 inches
Take time to check gauge.

PATTERN NOTE
Body of jacket is worked in one piece to armhole.

Instructions

BODY
Row 1 (RS): Starting at bottom with A, ch 87 [99, 111, 123, 135], sc in 2nd ch from hook and each ch across, turn. (*86 [98, 110, 122, 134] sc*)

Rows 2–34 [38, 42, 46, 50]: Ch 1, sc in each st across, turn.

LEFT FRONT
Row 1 (RS): Ch 1, sc in first 18 [21, 24, 27, 30] sc, turn, leaving rem sts unworked.

Rows 2–11 [15, 19, 23, 27]: Ch 1, sc in each st across, turn.

Row 12 [16, 20, 24, 28]: Ch 1, sc in each st to last st, turn, leaving last st unworked. (*17 [20, 23, 26, 29] sc*)

Note: *Mark unworked st for placement of front border.*

Row 13 [17, 21, 25, 29]: Ch 1, sc in each st across, turn.

Rows 14 [18, 22, 26, 30]–25 [29, 33, 37, 41]: [Rep last 2 rows] 6 times. (*11 [14, 17, 20, 23] sc*)

Rows 26 [30, 34, 38, 42]–42 [46, 50, 54, 58]: Ch 1, sc in each st across, turn.

Fasten off, leaving an 8-inch length for sewing.

BACK
Row 1 (RS): Hold with RS facing, sk next 9 [10, 11, 12, 13] sts from left front *(armhole)*, attach A with sc in next st, sc in next 31 [35, 39, 43, 47] sts, turn. (*32 [36, 40, 44, 48] sc*)

Row 2: Ch 1, 2 sc in first st *(inc)*, sc in each st to last st, 2 sc in last st *(inc)*, turn. (*34 [38, 42, 46, 50] sc*)

Row 3: Ch 1, sc in each st across, turn.

Rows 4–7: [Rep rows 2 and 3] twice. (*38 [42, 46, 50, 54] sc*)

Rows 8–25 [33, 41, 49, 57]: Ch 1, sc in each st across, turn.

Rows 26 [34, 42, 50, 58] & 27 [35, 43, 51, 59]: Ch 1, 2 sc in first st, sc in each st to last st, 2 sc in last st, turn. (*42 [46, 50, 54, 58] sc*)

Fasten off.

RIGHT FRONT
Row 1: Hold with RS facing, sk next 9 [10, 11, 12, 13] sts *(armhole)*, attach A with sc in next st, sc in each st across, turn. (*18 [21, 24, 27, 30] sc*)

Rows 2–11 [15, 19, 23, 27]: Ch 1, sc in each st across, turn.

Row 12 [16, 20, 24, 28]: Ch 1, sk first st, sc in each st across, ch 1, turn. (*17 [20, 23, 26, 29] sc*)

Note: *Mark sk st for placement of border.*

Row 13 [17, 21, 25, 29]: Ch 1, sc in each st across, turn.

Rows 14 [18, 22, 26, 30]–25 [29, 33, 37, 41]: [Rep rows 12 and 13] 7 times. (*10 [13, 16, 19, 22] sc*)

Rows 26 [30, 34, 38, 42]–42 [46, 50, 54, 58]: Ch 1, sc in each st across, turn.

Fasten off, leaving a 8-inch end for sewing.

ASSEMBLY
Matching sts, sew last row of left and right sides to back.

RIGHT FRONT BAND
FIRST SIDE
Row 1: Hold piece with RS of Right Front facing, working in ends of rows, attach A with sc in first row, sc in each row of body and to marked st, turn. (*46 [54, 62, 70, 78] sc*)

Row 2: Ch 3 (*counts as a dc*), dc in each st across, turn.

Row 3: Ch 1, sc in each st across, turn.

Rows 4 & 5: Rep row 3.

Fasten off.

LEFT FRONT BAND
Row 1: Hold piece with RS of Left Front facing, working in ends of rows, attach A in marked st, sc in each row to first row, turn. (*46 [54, 62, 70, 78] sc*)

Row 2: Ch 3 (*counts as a dc*), dc in each st across, turn.

Row 3: Ch 1, sc in each st across, turn.

Rows 4 & 5: Rep row 3.

NECK EDGING

Note: *For* **sc dec,** *draw up lp in each of 2 sts indicated, yo and draw through all 3 lps on hook.*

Row 1: With A, join with sc in end of last row of Right Front Band, sc in end of each row of Band, working along Right Front neck edge, **sc dec** (*see Note*) in next 2 sts, sc evenly spaced along Right Front neck edge, in sts across Back and along Left Front edge to last 2 sts before Left Front Band, sc dec in last 2 sts, sc in end of each row of Left Front Band, turn.

Row 2: Ch 1, sc in each st across, changing to 2 strands of B in last sc.

Row 3: Ch 1, sc in each st across, turn.

Row 4: Ch 3 (*counts as a dc*), dc in each st across, turn.

Row 5: Ch 1, sc in each st across.

Fasten off.

SLEEVE
Note: *For **sc dec,** draw up lp in each of 2 rows indicated, yo and draw through all 3 lps on hook.*

For X-Small Size Only
Rnd 1: Attach A with sc in first sk st of 1 armhole, sc in next 8 sts, working in row ends around opening; [**sc dec** (*see Note*) in next 2 rows] 4 times, [sc in next 11 rows, sc dec] twice, sc in next row, [sc dec, sc in next 11 rows] twice, [sc dec] 4 times, join with sl st in first sc. (*66 sc*)

Rnd 2: Ch 1, sc in each st dec 4 sts evenly spaced around, join with sl st in first sc. (*62 sc*)

Rnd 3: Ch 1, sc in each st, join with sl st in first sc.

Rnds 4 & 5: Rep rnd 3.

[Rep rnds 2–5] 8 times. (*30 sts*)

Next rnd: Ch 1, sc in each st; join with sl st in first sc.

Rep last rnd to desired length.

Fasten off.

For Small Size Only
Rnd 1: Attach A with sc in first sk st of 1 armhole, sc in next 9 sts, working in row ends around opening; [**sc dec** (*see Note*) in next 2 rows] 4 times, [sc in next 11 rows, sc dec] twice, sc in next 4 rows,

sc dec, sc in next row, sc dec, sc in next 4 rows, [sc dec, sc in next 11 rows] twice, [sc dec] 4 times, join with sl st in first sc. (*77 sc*)

Rnd 2: Ch 1, sc in each st dec 5 sts evenly spaced around, join with sl st in first sc. (*72 sc*)

Rnd 3: Ch 1, sc in each st, join with sl st in first sc.

Rnds 4 & 5: Rep rnd 3.

[Rep rnds 2–5] 8 times. (*32 sts*)

Next rnd: Ch 1, sc in each st; join with sl st in fist sc.

Rep last rnd to desired length.

Fasten off.

For Medium Size Only
Rnd 1: Attach A with sc in first sk st of 1 armhole, sc in next 10 sts, working in row ends around opening; [**sc dec** (*see Note*) in next 2 rows] 4 times, [sc in next 11 rows, sc dec] twice, sc in next 5 rows, sc dec, sc in next 5 rows, [sc dec, sc in next 11 rows] twice, [sc dec] 4 times, join with sl st in first sc. (*90 sc*)

Rnd 2: Ch 1, sc in each st dec 6 sts evenly spaced around, join with sl st in first sc. (*84 sc*)

Rnd 3: Ch 1, sc in each st, join with sl st in first sc.

Rnds 4 & 5: Rep rnd 3.

[Rep rnds 2–5] 8 times. (*36 sts*)

Next rnd: Ch 1, sc in each st, dec 2 sts evenly spaced around; join with sl st in first sc. (*34 sts*)

Next rnd: Ch 1, sc in each st; join with sl st in first sc.

Rep last rnd to desired length.

Fasten off.

For Large Size Only
Rnd 1: Attach A with sc in first sk st of 1 armhole, sc in next 11 sts, working in row ends around opening; [**sc dec** (*see Note*) in next 2 rows] 4 times, [sc in next 11 rows, sc dec] 7 times, [sc dec] 3 times, join with sl st in first sc. (*103 sc*)

Rnd 2: Ch 1, sc in each st dec 7 sts evenly spaced around, join with sl st in first sc. (*96 sc*)

Rnd 3: Ch 1, sc in each st, join with sl st in first sc.

Rnds 4 & 5: Rep rnd 3.

[Rep rnds 2–5] 9 times. (*33 sts*)

Next rnd: Ch 1, sc in each st; join with sl st in first sc.

Rep last rnd to desired length.

Fasten off.

For X-Large Size Only
Rnd 1: Attach A with sc in first sk st of 1 armhole, sc in next 12 sts, working in row ends around opening; [**sc dec** *(see Note)* in next 2 rows] 4 times, [sc in next 11 rows, sc dec] 3 times, sc in next 10 rows, sc dec, sc in next row, sc dec, sc in next 10 rows, [sc dec, sc in next 11 rows] 3 times, [sc dec] 4 times, join with sl st in first sc. *(116 sc)*

Rnd 2: Ch 1, sc in each st dec 8 sts evenly spaced around, join with sl st in first sc. *(108 sc)*

Rnd 3: Ch 1, sc in each st, join with sl st in first sc.

Rnds 4 & 5: Rep rnd 3.

[Rep rnds 2–5] 9 times. *(36 sts)*

Next rnd: Ch 1, sc in each st; join with sl st in first sc.

Rep last rnd to desired length.

Fasten off.

SLEEVE TRIM
Rnd 1: With 2 strands of B held tog, make slip knot on hook and join with sc in any st of last rnd, ch 1, (sc, ch 1) in each st around, join with sl st in first sc.

Rnd 2: Sl st in first ch-1 sp, ch 3 *(counts as dc)*, dc in same sp, 2 dc in each ch-1 sp around, join with sl st in 3rd ch of beg ch-3. Fasten off.

Rep for other Sleeve.

LOWER TRIM
Row 1: With 2 strands of B held tog and working in edge sts of Front Band, join with sc in first row of Left Front Band, sc in each row of Band, in unused lps of beg ch and in end of each row of Right Front Band, turn.

Row 2: Ch 3 *(counts as a dc)*, dc in each st across, turn.

Row 3: Ch 3, dc in each st across.

Fasten off.

FINISHING
Sew side seams.

With sewing needle and matching thread, sew frog closure to Front Band below neck trim. ❦

Quick & Easy Nouveau Shrug

DESIGN BY NANCY NEHRING

SKILL LEVEL  EASY

FINISHED SIZES
Instructions given fit woman's small; changes for medium and large are in [ ].

FINISHED GARMENT MEASUREMENTS
Chest: 66 x 13 inches [70 x 15 inches, 74 x 17 inches]

MATERIALS
 Lion Brand Moonlight Mohair bulky (chunky) weight yarn (1¾ oz/82 yds/50g per ball): 5 [6, 7] balls #201 rain forest *(A)*
 Lion Brand Lion Suede bulky (chunky) weight yarn (3 oz/122 yds/85g per ball): 1 ball #126 coffee *(B)*
Size N/13/9mm crochet hook or size needed to obtain gauge
Size K/10½/6.5mm crochet hook
Yarn needle

GAUGE
With smaller hook: 4½ esc = 4 inches; 5½ rows = 4 inches
Take time to check gauge.

SPECIAL STITCH
Extended single crochet (**esc**): Insert hook in st indicated, yo, pull up lp, yo, draw through 1 lp on hook, yo, draw through 2 lps on hook.

Instructions

BACK
With larger hook and A, ch 75 [80, 85].

Row 1: Ch 1, **esc** (*see Special Stitch*) in each ch across, turn.

Row 2: Ch 1, esc in each st across, turn.

Rows 3–18 [21, 24]: Rep row 2.

Fasten off.

ASSEMBLY
Seam shoulders as shown in Fig.1.

BODY EDGING
Rnd 1: With smaller hook and B, attach yarn with sc to lower edge of center Back, ch 2, *[sc in next st, ch 1] to st before shoulder seam, [yo, pull up lp in next st] twice, yo, draw through all 3 lps on hook, ch 1; rep from * once more, [sc in next st, ch 1] to joining; join with sl st in first sc.

Rnd 2: Ch 2, *sc in next ch-1 sp, ch 1; rep from * around, join in first sc.

Fasten off.

ARMHOLE EDGING
Rnd 1: With smaller hook and B, attach yarn with sc to one armhole opening, ch 2, *[sc in next st, ch 1] around; join with sl st in first sc.

Rnd 2: Ch 2, *sc in next ch-1 sp, ch 1; rep from * around, join in first sc.

Fasten off.

Rep for other armhole opening. 🌱

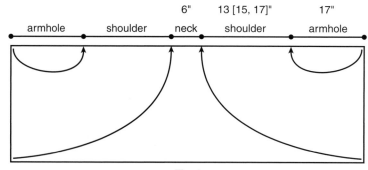

Fig. 1

Snuggle-Up Afghans

These afghans add texture and coziness to a
room while offering needed warmth so the
thermostat can stay a little lower.

Lush & Luxurious Log Cabin Afghan

DESIGN BY BONNIE PIERCE

SKILL LEVEL ■□□□
BEGINNER

FINISHED SIZE
Approximately 47 x 50 inches

MATERIALS
 Red Heart Super Saver medium (worsted) weight yarn:
8 oz/ 452 yds/224g each #385 royal blue *(A)* and #886 blue *(C)*

 Red Heart Bright and Lofty super bulky (super chunky) weight yarn:
12 oz/285 yds/336g #9955 beach *(B)*

 Lion Brand Homespun bulky (chunky) weight yarn:
16 oz/493 yds/448g #368 Montana sky *(D)*

Lion Brand Fun Fur bulky (chunky) weight eyelash yarn:
8¾ oz/300 yds/245g #109 sapphire *(E)*

Size N/13/9mm crochet hook or size needed to obtain gauge
Tapestry needle

GAUGE
7 dc = 3 inches

PATTERN NOTE
Afghan is worked from center outward.

Instructions

AFGHAN
Row 1 (RS): With A, ch 18, dc in 4th ch from hook and in each ch across, turn. (*16 dc*)

Row 2: Ch 2, dc in each st across, turn.

Row 3: Ch 2, dc in each st across, changing to B in last st. Do not turn.

Row 4: Ch 2, working across end of rows, 2 dc in end of each row, turn. (*6 dc*)

Row 5: Ch 2, dc in each st across, turn.

Row 6: Ch 2, dc in each st across, changing to C in last st. Do not turn.

Row 7: Ch 2, working across ends of last 3 rows, 2 dc in end of each row, working in unused lps of beg ch, dc in each of next 16 lps, turn. (*22 dc*)

Row 8: Ch 2, dc in each st across, turn.

Row 9: Ch 2, dc in each st across, changing to D in last st. Do not turn.

Row 10: Ch 2, working in ends of last 3 rows, 2 dc in end of each row, 2 dc in end of each of next 3 rows, turn. (*12 dc*)

Row 11: Ch 2, dc in each st across, turn.

Row 12: Ch 2, dc in each st across, changing to E in last st. Do not turn.

Row 13: Ch 2, working in ends of last 3 rows, 2 dc in end of each row, dc in next 16 sts, 2 dc in end of each of next 3 rows, turn. (*28 dc*)

Row 14: Ch 2, dc in each st across, turn.

Row 15: Ch 2, dc in each st across, changing to A in last st. Do not turn.

CONTINUED ON PAGE 125

Modern Day Warmth Sofa Afghan

DESIGN BY ZELDA WORKMAN

SKILL LEVEL

FINISHED SIZE
Approximately 54 x 66 inches

MATERIALS
 Red Heart Plush medium (worsted)
weight yarn:
24 oz/1160 yds/672g each #9628 dark sage
(A) and #9104 taupe *(B)*
Size H/8/5mm crochet hook or size needed to
obtain gauge
Tapestry needle

GAUGE
13 sts = 4 inches

SPECIAL STITCHES
Beginning extended stitch (beg e-st): Yo, insert
hook in next ch-1 sp, pull up a lp, working around
ch-1 sts made in previous rows, [yo, insert hook
from front to back around ch st of row below, pull
up a lp] 10 times, yo, insert hook from front to back
around ch st of foundation ch, pull up a lp, [yo, pull
through 2 lps on hook] 22 times.

Extended stitch (e-st): Yo, insert hook in next ch-1
sp, pull up a lp, working around ch-1 sts made in
previous rows, [yo, insert hook from front to back
around ch st of row below, pull up a lp] 8 times, yo,
insert hook in top of e-st in next row, pull up a lp,
inset hook around post of same e-st, pull up a lp,
[yo, pull through 2 lps on hook] 22 times.

Instructions

AFGHAN
CENTER
Row 1 (RS): With B, ch 166, dc in 4th ch from hook
and in next 2 chs, [ch 1, sk next ch, dc in next 4 ch]
across, turn. (*163 sts*)

Row 2: Ch 3 (*counts as a dc now and throughout*),
dc in next 3 dc, [ch 1, sk next ch, dc in next 4 dc]
across, turn.

Rows 3–10: Rep row 2, changing to A at end of
row 10.

Row 11: Ch 3, dc in next 3 dc, [**beg e-st** (*see
Special Stitches*) over next vertical row of ch-1 sps,
dc in next 4 dc] across, turn.

Row 12: Ch 3, dc in next 3 dc, [ch 1, sk next e-st,
dc in next 4 dc] across, turn.

Rows 13–20: Rep row 2, changing to B at end of
row 20.

Row 21: Ch 3, dc in next 3 dc, [**e-st** (*see Special
Stitches*) over next vertical row of ch-1 sps, dc in
next 4 dc] across, turn.

Row 22: Ch 3, dc in next 3 dc, [ch 1, sk next e-st,
dc in next 4 dc] across, turn.

Rows 23–30: Rep row 2, changing to A at end of
row 30.

Rows 31–110: Rep rows 21–30, changing color
at end of every 10th row. Change to A at end of
row 110.

Row 111: Ch 3, dc in next 3 dc, *e-st over next
vertical row of ch-1 sps, dc in next 4 dc, rep from
* to last ch-1 sp, e-st over last vertical row of ch-1
sps, dc in next 3 dc, 3 dc in last dc, turn.

BORDER
Working along side of Afghan, 2 dc in end of each
row to next corner, 3 dc in first st of foundation ch,
dc in each st to last st of foundation ch, 3 dc in
last st, 2 dc in end of each row to next corner, 2 dc
in same st as beg ch-3 of row 111, sl st in top of
beg ch-3.

Fasten off and weave in all ends. ❧

Spirals to Surround You Afghan

DESIGN BY LISA PFLUG

SKILL LEVEL  BEGINNER

FINISHED SIZE
Approximately 46 x 67 inches

MATERIALS
 Lion Brand Homespun bulky (chunky)
weight yarn:
42 oz/1295 yds/1176g #322 baroque (A)
 Lion Brand Suede bulky (chunky) weight yarn:
6 oz/244 yds/168g each #147 eggplant (B)
and #146 fuchsia (C)
Size J/10/6mm crochet hook or size needed to
obtain gauge
Stitch markers
Tapestry needle

GAUGE
9 dc = 4 inches

Instructions

SPIRAL MOTIF
Make 12.
With A, ch 4, sl st to form a ring.

Note: *Rnds 1–5 are worked in continuous rnds. Do not join; mark beg of rnds.*

Rnd 1 (RS): In ring, work (sc, 2 hdc, 9 dc). (*12 sts*)

Rnd 2: Working in **back lps** (*see Stitch Guide*) only, 2 dc in next sc, 2 dc in each rem st. (*24 sts*)

Rnd 3: Working in back lps only, 2 dc in next dc, dc in next st, [2 dc in next st, dc in next st] around. (*36 sts*)

Rnd 4: Working in back lps only, 2 dc in next dc, dc in next 2 sts, [2 dc in next st, dc in next 2 sts] around. (*48 sts*)

Rnd 5: Working in back lps only, 2 dc in next dc, dc in next 3 sts, [2 dc in next st, dc in next 3 sts] around, join with sl st in first dc. (*60 sts*)

Fasten off.

Rnd 6: Hold Motif with last st at bottom, join B with sl st to **front lp** (*see Stitch Guide*) of last st, working in front lps only and from outside of Motif toward center, sl st loosely in front lps until reaching center.

Fasten off and pull loose end through center of Motif.

Note: *For each Motif, join yarn on following rnd at a different point of spiral so they are oriented randomly.*

Rnd 7: With RS facing, join A with sc to back lp of any st on row 5, sc each st around, join with sl st in first sc.

Rnd 8: *Sc in next 2 sts, hdc in next 2 sts, dc in next 2 sts, tr in next st, 5 tr in next st—corner made, tr in next st, dc in next 2 sts, hdc in next 2 sts, sc in next 2 st, rep from * 3 times more, join.

Rnd 9: Ch 3, *dc in each st to 3rd dc of next corner, 5 dc in 3rd dc, rep from * 3 times more, dc in each st across, join with sl st in top of beg ch-3.

Fasten off and weave in all ends.

STRIPE MOTIF
Make 12.
Row 1: With A, ch 26, dc in 4th ch from hook and in each ch across, turn. (*24 dc*)

Row 2: Ch 3 (*counts as a dc now and throughout*), dc in each st across, turn. Fasten off.

Row 3: Join C with a sc in first st, sc in each st across, turn.

Row 4: Ch 1, sc in each st across, turn. Fasten off.

Row 5: Join A with sl st in first st, ch 3, dc in each st across, turn.

Row 6: Ch 3, dc in each st across, turn. Fasten off.

Row 7: Join B with a sc in first st, sc in each st across, turn. Fasten off.

Row 8: Join C with a sc in first st, sc in each st across, turn.

Row 9: Ch 1, sc in each st across, turn.

Rows 10 & 11: Rep row 9. Fasten off.

Row 12: Rep row 7.

Rows 13 & 14: Rep rows 5 and 6.

Rows 15–18: Rep rows 3–6.

Fasten off and weave in all ends.

ASSEMBLY
Referring to diagram for placement of motifs and with A, sew motifs tog in 6 rows of 4 motifs each.

EDGING
Row 1: With RS facing, join A with sl st to any corner, ch 3, 4 dc in same sp, *dc in each st to next corner, 5 dc in corner, rep from * twice more, dc in each st across, join with sl st in top of ch-3. Fasten off.

Row 2: With RS facing, join B with a sc to 3rd dc of any corner, 2 sc in same st, *sc in each st to 3rd dc of next corner, 3 sc in 3rd dc, rep from * twice more, sc in each st across, join with sl st in first sc.

Fasten off and weave in all ends. ❦

Spirals to Surround You

Lush & Luxurious Log
Cabin Afghan CONTINUED FROM PAGE 118

CONTINUED FROM PAGE 118

Row 16: Ch 2, working in ends of last 3 rows, 2 dc in end of each row, dc in next 6 sts, 2 dc in end of each of next 3 rows, turn. *(18 sts)*

Row 17: Ch 2, dc in each st across, turn.

Row 18: Ch 2, dc in each st across, changing to B in last st. Do not turn.

Row 19: Ch 2, working in ends of last 3 rows, 2 dc in end of each row, dc in each st across, 2 dc in end of each of next 3 rows, turn.

Row 20: Ch 2, dc in each st across, turn.

Row 21: Ch 2, dc in each st across, changing to C in last st. Do not turn.

Row 22: Ch 2, working in ends of last 3 rows, 2 dc in end of each row, dc in each st across, 2 dc in end of each of next 3 rows, turn.

Row 23: Ch 2, dc in each st across, turn.

Row 24: Ch 2, dc in each st across, changing to D in last st. Do not turn.

Row 25: Ch 2, working in ends of last 3 rows, 2 dc in end of each row, dc in each st across, 2 dc in end of each of next 3 rows, turn.

Row 26: Ch 2, dc in each st across, turn.

Row 27: Ch 2, dc in each st across, changing to E in last st. Do not turn.

Row 28: Ch 2, working in ends of last 3 rows, 2 dc in end of each row, dc in each st across, 2 dc in end of each of next 3 rows, turn.

Row 29: Ch 2, dc in each st across, turn.

Rows 30–89: [Work rows 15–29] 4 times.

Row 90: Ch 2, dc in each st across, do not turn, do not change color.

Row 91: Ch 2, working in ends of last 3 rows, 2 dc in each row, dc in each st across, 2 dc in end of each of next 3 rows, turn.

Row 92: Ch 2, dc in each st across, turn.

Row 93: Ch 2, dc in each st across. Do not turn.

Rows 94–99: [Work rows 91–93] twice.

Fasten off and weave in all ends. ❦

Warm-Up With Ripples Afghan

DESIGN BY CINDY ADAMS

SKILL LEVEL EASY

FINISHED SIZE
Approximately 52 x 62 inches

MATERIALS

 Bernat Soft Boucle bulky (chunky)
weight yarn:
10 oz/510 yds/280g each #06163 dark rose
(A), #06903 blooming rose *(B)* and #22425
soft rose *(C)*

 Patons ChaCha super bulky (super chunky)
weight yarn:
7 oz/308 yds/196g #02016 raggae *(D)*
Size J/10/6mm crochet hook or size needed to
obtain gauge
Tapestry needle

GAUGE
Two 3-dc groups = 2 inches

PATTERN NOTE
Color sequence is as follows: 3 rows A (do not count
row 1 or last row), 3 rows B, 3 rows C, 2 rows D.

SPECIAL STITCH
Cluster (cl): Keeping last lp of each dc on hook,
3 dc in sp indicated, yo and draw through all 4 lps
on hook.

Instructions

**AFGHAN
CENTER
Row 1 (RS):** With A, ch 140 loosely, sc in 2nd ch
from hook and in each ch across, turn. (*139 sc*)

Row 2: Ch 2, sk first 3 sc, [3 dc in next sc, sk next
2 sc] 3 times, in next sc work (3 dc, ch 3, 3 dc),
*[sk next 2 sc, 3 dc in next sc] twice, sk next 2 sc,
cl (*see Special Stitch*) in next sc, sk next 4 sc, cl in
next sc, [sk next 2 sc, 3 dc in next sc] twice, sk next
2 sc, in next sc work (3 dc, ch 3, 3 dc), rep from * to
last 12 sc, sk next 2 sc, [3 dc in next sc, sk next 2
sc] 3 times, dc in last sc, turn.

Row 3: Ch 2, sk first sp (between turning ch and
next 3-dc group), 3 dc in next 3 sps (between each
3-dc group), in next ch-3 sp work (3 dc, ch 3, 3 dc),
*3 dc in next 2 sps, cl in next sp, sk sp between
cls, cl in next sp, 3 dc in next 2 sps, in next ch-3 sp
work (3 dc, ch 3, 3 dc), rep from * to last 4 sps, 3
dc in next 3 sps, dc in last sp, turn.

Following color sequence, rep row 3 for 65 inches,
ending last rep with 3 rows of A.

Next row: Ch 1, sc in each dc and 3 sc in each ch-
3 sp across.

Fasten off and weave in all ends.

The Heat's on Hexagon Afghan

DESIGN BY ELLEN GORMLEY

SKILL LEVEL ●☐☐☐
BEGINNER

FINISHED SIZE
Approximately 55 x 70 inches

MATERIALS
 Red Heart Super Saver medium (worsted) weight yarn:
48 oz/2,712 yds/1,344g #316 soft white *(A)*
 TLC Essentials medium (worsted) weight yarn:
12 oz/652 yds/336g #2913 ranch red *(B)*
 Moda Dea Fur Ever bulky (chunky) weight yarn:
12³⁄₁₀ oz/343 yds/345g #3926 red hot *(C)*
Size I/9/5.5mm crochet hook or size needed to obtain gauge
Tapestry needle

GAUGE
Hexagon = 10 inches from point to point

PATTERN NOTE
Join with slip stitch in first stitch unless otherwise indicated.

SPECIAL STITCH
Puff stitch (puff st): (Yo, draw up lp in st indicated) 5 times, yo and draw through all 11 lps on hook.

Instructions

HEXAGON
Make 53.
With A, ch 4, join with sl st to form a ring.

Rnd 1 (RS): Ch 1, 6 sc in ring, join. (*6 sc*)

Rnd 2: Ch 1, 2 sc in first sc and each sc around, join. (*12 sc*)

Rnd 3: Ch 1, sc in first sc, 2 sc in next sc, [sc in next sc, 2 sc in next sc] 5 times, join. (*18 sc*)

Rnd 4: Ch 1, working in **back lps** (*see Stitch Guide*) only, sc in first sc and in next sc, 2 sc in next sc, [sc in next 2 sc, 2 sc in next sc] 5 times, join in both lps of first sc. (*24 sc*)

Rnd 5: Ch 1, sc in first sc and in next 2 sc, 2 sc in next sc, [sc in next 3 sc, 2 sc in next sc] 5 times, join. (*30 sc*)

Rnd 6: Ch 1, sc in first sc and in next 3 sc, 2 sc in next sc, [sc in next 4 sc, 2 sc in next sc] 5 times, join. (*36 sc*)

Rnd 7: Ch 1, sc in first sc and in next 4 sc, 2 sc in next sc, [sc in next 5 sc, 2 sc in next sc] 5 times, join. (*42 sc*)

Rnd 8: Ch 1, sc in first sc and in next 5 sc, 2 sc in next sc, [sc in next 6 sc, 2 sc in next sc] 5 times, join. (*48 sc*)

Rnd 9: Ch 1, working in **front lps** (*see Stitch Guide*) only, sc in first sc and in each sc around, join in both lps of first sc. (*48 sc*)

CONTINUED ON PAGE 139

Layer of Luxury Comfort Afghan

DESIGN BY JACQUELINE STETTER

SKILL LEVEL EASY

FINISHED SIZE
Approximately 52 x 65 inches

MATERIALS
 Red Heart Plush medium (worsted) weight yarn:
    32 oz/1,547 yds/896g #9627 light sage *(A)*
    27 oz/1,305 yds/756g #9995 marina print *(B)*
Size N/13/9mm crochet hook or size needed to
    obtain gauge
Tapestry needle

GAUGE
7 dc = 3 inches

Instructions

AFGHAN
CENTER
Row 1 (RS): With 1 strand each A and B, ch 103, dc in 3rd ch from hook *(beg 2 sk chs count as a dc)* and in each ch across, turn. *(101 dc)*

Row 2: Ch 2 *(counts as a dc)*, dc in each dc across.

Rep row 2 until piece measures approximately 60 inches.

Fasten off and weave in all ends.

BORDER
Rnd 1: With RS facing and A, join with sl st in beg corner, ch 2 *(counts as a hdc now and through-out)*, hdc in each st across to next corner, 3 hdc in corner, hdc evenly spaced along side to next corner, 3 hdc in corner, hdc in each dc across to next corner, 3 hdc in corner, hdc evenly spaced along side to next corner, 2 hdc in corner, join with sl st in first hdc.

Rnd 2: Ch 2, hdc in each hdc around, working 3 hdc in center hdc of each corner, join.

Rnd 3: Rep row 2.

Rnd 4: [Ch 4, sk next hdc, sc in next hdc] around, join with sl st in top of ch-4. Fasten off.

Rnd 5: Join B with sl st in next open hdc on rnd 3, [ch 4, working in front of ch-4 made by A on rnd 4, sc in next open hdc, ch 4, working in back of next ch-4, sc in next open hdc] around, join.

Fasten off and weave in all ends. 🐛

Hot! Hot! Hot! Fiesta Throw

DESIGN BY CINDY ADAMS

SKILL LEVEL
BEGINNER

FINISHED SIZE
Approximately 53 x 70 inches

MATERIALS
 Lion Brand Wool Ease medium (worsted)
weight yarn:
3 oz/197 yds/84g #102 ranch red *(A)*
12 oz/788 yds/336g #147 purple *(E)*
 Lion Brand Fun Fur bulky (chunky) weight
eyelash yarn:
7 oz/240 yds/196g #191 violet *(B)*
12¼ oz/420 yds/343g #194 lime *(D)*
 Lion Brand Pound of Love medium (worsted)
weight yarn:
16 oz/1,020 yds/448g each #148 turquoise
(C) and #102 bubblegum *(F)*
Size I/9/5.5mm crochet hook or size needed to
obtain gauge
Tapestry needle

GAUGE
Square = 8¾ inches

SPECIAL STITCHES
Beginning popcorn (beg pc): Ch 3, 3 dc in sp
indicated, remove lp from hook, insert hook in top of
beg ch-3, pull dropped lp through.

Popcorn (pc): 4 dc in sp indicted, remove lp
from hook, insert hook in first dc, pull dropped
lp through.

Instructions

THROW
CENTER
Make 48 squares.
With A, ch 6, join to form a ring.

Rnd 1 (RS): Work **beg pc** (*see Special Stitches*) in
ring, ch 3, [**pc** (*see Special Stitches*) in ring, ch 3]
3 times, join with sl st in top of beg pc. (*4 ch-3 sps*)
Fasten off.

Rnd 2: With RS facing, join B with sl st in any ch-3
sp, [beg pc, ch 3, pc] in same sp, ch 3, [pc, ch 3]
twice in each ch-3 sp around, join with sl st in top of
beg pc. (*8 ch-3 sps*)

Fasten off.

Rnd 3: With C, rep rnd 2. (*16 ch-3 sps*)

Rnd 4: With RS facing, join D with sl st in any ch-3
sp, (ch 3, 2 dc, ch 3, 3 dc) in same sp, ch 1, *[3 dc
in next ch-3 sp, ch 1] 3 times, (3 dc, ch 3, 3 dc) in
next ch-3 sp, rep from * around, ch 1, join with sl st
in top of ch-3. Fasten off.

Rnd 5: With RS facing, join E with sl st in any corner
ch-3 sp, (ch 3, 2 dc, ch 3, 3 dc) in same sp, ch 1,
*[3 dc in next ch-1 sp, ch 1] 4 times, (3 dc, ch 3, 3
dc) in next ch-3 sp, rep from * around, ch 1, join.
Fasten off.

Rnd 6: With RS facing, join F with sl st in any corner
ch-3 sp, (ch 3, 2 dc, ch 3, 3 dc) in same sp, *[3 dc
in next ch-1 sp] 5 times, (3 dc, ch 3, 3 dc) in next
ch-3 sp, rep from * around, ch 1, join.

Fasten off and weave in all ends.

ASSEMBLY
Join squares in 8 rows of 6 squares each. To join,
hold squares with WS tog. With F and working in
back lps (*see Stitch Guide*) only, sc squares tog,
beg and ending in corner ch-3 sps.

FINISHING
Hold afghan with RS facing and 1 short end at top.
Join F in ch-3 sp in upper right-hand corner, ch 1,
3 sc in same sp, *sc in each st across to next corner
ch-3 sp, 3 sc in ch-3 sp; rep from * twice more; sc in
each st to first sc, join with sl st in first sc.

Fasten off and weave in ends.

My Blue Denim Wrap Afghan

DESIGN BY EDIE ECKMAN

SKILL LEVEL
EASY

FINISHED SIZE
Approximately 39 x 54 inches

MATERIALS
Patons Divine bulky (chunky) weight yarn: 31½ oz/1,278 yds/882g #06117 denim storm
Size M/13/9mm crochet hook or size needed to obtain gauge
Tapestry needle

GAUGE
7 sts = 4 inches

SPECIAL STITCHES
Back post double crochet (bpdc): Yo, insert hook from back to front around **post** *(see Stitch Guide)*

of next st, yo, draw lp through, [yo, draw through 2 lps on hook] twice.

Front post double crochet (fpdc): Yo, insert hook from front to back around **post** *(see Stitch Guide)* of next st, yo, draw lp through, [yo, draw through 2 lps on hook] twice.

Instructions

AFGHAN
Row 1 (RS): Ch 76, dc in 3rd ch from hook and in each ch across, turn. (*74 sts*)

Row 2: Ch 2 *(counts as a dc now and throughout)*, **fpdc** *(see Special Stitches)* around next 2 st, **bpdc** *(see Special Stitches)* around next st [fpdc around next 3 sts, bpdc around next st] across to last 3 sts, fpdc around next 2 sts, dc in 2nd ch of beg ch-2, turn.

Row 3: Ch 2, dc in next 2 sts, [fpdc around next st, dc in next 3 st] across, ending with a dc in 2nd ch of turning ch-2, turn.

Row 4: Ch 2, fpdc around next 2 sts, bpdc around next st, [fpdc around next 3 sts, bpdc around next st] across to last 3 sts, fpdc around next 2 sts, dc in 2nd ch of turning ch-2, turn.

Rep rows 3 and 4 until piece measures approximately 54 inches, ending with row 3.

Fasten off and weave in all ends.

Cozy & Cuddly Mitered Afghan

DESIGN BY BONNIE PIERCE

SKILL LEVEL ■□□□
BEGINNER

FINISHED SIZE
Approximately 48 x 65 inches

MATERIALS

 Red Heart Super Saver medium (worsted) weight yarn:
8 oz/452 yds/224g #365 coffee *(A)*

 Lion Brand Homespun bulky (chunky) weight yarn:
12 oz/370 yds/336g #309 deco *(B)*
6 oz/185 yds/168g each #311 rococo *(D)* and #326 ranch *(E)*

Red Heart Kiss bulky (chunky) weight yarn:
7 oz/332 yds/200g #3546 smoke *(C)*

Lion Brand Polarspun bulky (chunky) weight yarn:
1¾ oz/137 yds/49g #100 snow white *(F)*

Lion Brand Moonlight Mohair bulky (chunky) weight yarn:
5½ oz/246 yds/147g #203 safari *(G)*

Size N/13/9mm crochet hook or size needed to obtain gauge

Tapestry needle

GAUGE
Square = 8 inches

Instructions

FIRST ROW
FIRST SQUARE
Note: *First Square is square in lower right-hand corner of afghan.*

Row 1 (RS): With A, ch 39, sc in 2nd ch from hook and in each ch across, turn. *(38 sc)*

Note: *For **sc dec,** pull up lp in each of 2 sts indicated, yo and draw through all 3 lps on hook.*

Row 2: Ch 1, sc in first 17 sts, [**sc dec** (*see Note*) in next 2 sts] twice, sc in next 17 sts, changing to B in last st, turn.

Row 3: Ch 1, sc in first 16 sts, [sc dec] twice, sc in next 16 sts, turn.

Row 4: Ch 1, sc in first 15 sts, [sc dec] twice, sc in next 15 sts, changing to C in last st, turn.

Row 5: Ch 1, sc in first 14 sts, [sc dec] twice, sc in next 14 sts, turn.

Row 6: Ch 1, sc in first 13 sts, [sc dec] twice, sc in next 13 sts, changing to D in last st, turn.

Row 7: Ch 1, sc in first 12 sts, [sc dec] twice, sc in next 12 sts, turn.

Row 8: Ch 1, sc in first 11 sts, [sc dec] twice, sc in next 11 sts, changing to E in last st, turn.

Row 9: Ch 1, sc in first 10 sts, [sc dec] twice, sc in next 10 sts, turn.

Row 10: Ch 1, sc in first 9 sts, [sc dec] twice, sc in next 9 sts, changing to F in last st, turn.

Row 11: Ch 1, sc in next 8 sts, [sc dec] twice, sc in next 8 sts, turn.

Row 12: Ch 1, sc in first 7 sts, [sc dec] twice, sc in next 7 sts, changing to G in last st, turn.

Row 13: Ch 1, sc in first 6 sts, [sc dec] twice, sc in next 6 sts, turn.

Row 14: Ch 1, sc in first 5 sts, [sc dec] twice, sc in next 5 sts, changing to B in last st, turn.

Row 15: Ch 1, sc in first 4 sts, [sc dec] twice, sc in next 4 sts, turn.

Row 16: Ch 1, sc in first 3 sts, [sc dec] twice, sc in next 3 sts, changing to A in last st, turn.

Row 17: Ch 1, sc in first 2 sts, [sc dec] twice, sc in next 2 sts, turn.

Row 18: Ch 1, sc in first st, [sc dec] twice, sc in next st, turn.

Row 19: [Sc dec] twice, turn.

Row 20: Ch 1, sc dec, turn.

2ND SQUARE
Row 1 (RS): Ch 1, work 19 sc across side of completed square, ch 20, turn.

Row 2: Sc in 2nd ch from hook and in next 16 chs, [sc dec in next 2 sts] twice, sc in next 17 sts, changing to B in last st, turn.

Rows 3–20: Rep rows 3–20 of First Square.

3RD & 4TH SQUARES
Work same as 2nd Square.

5TH SQUARE
Work same as 2nd Square through row 20.

Edging row: Work 19 sc across side of completed square.

Fasten off and weave in all ends.

2ND ROW
FIRST SQUARE
Row 1 (RS): With A, ch 20, sc in 2nd ch from hook and in each ch across, sc in 19 sts across top of First Square in First Row, turn.

Rows 2–20: Rep rows 2–20 of First Square of First Row.

2ND SQUARE
Row 1 (RS): With A, work 19 sc across side of last completed square, sc in 19 sts across top of next square on row 1, turn.

Rows 2–20: Rep rows 2–20 of First Square of First Row.

3RD–5TH SQUARES
Work same as 2nd Square of 2nd Row.

3RD–7TH ROWS
Work same as 2nd Row.

Hold afghan with RS facing and 7th Row at top; join A in upper right-hand corner, ch 1, sc evenly across to end of last square of row. Fasten off.

BORDER
Rnd 1: With RS facing and 7th Row at top, join A in first sc in upper right-hand corner, ch 1, sc in same sc; sc in each sc across to last sc, 3 sc in last st, sc across next side to next corner, 3 sc in next corner, working across next side, sc across beg ch to last st, 3 sc in last st, sc across next side to first sc, join with sl st in first sc.

Rnd 2: Ch 1, sc in same sc, 3 sc in next sc, *sc in each sc to 2nd sc of next corner; 3 sc in 2nd sc; rep from * twice more, sc in each sc to first sc, join.

Fasten off and weave in all ends. ❦

The Heat's on Hexagon Afghan CONTINUED FROM PAGE 128

Rnd 10: With RS facing, working behind rnd 9 in unused lps of rnd 8, join A with an sc in any sc, sc in next 7 sc, ch 3, [sc in next 8 sc, ch 3] 5 times, join.

Rnd 11: Ch 3 (*counts as a dc now and throughout*), dc in next 2 sc, *ch 2, sk next 2 sc, dc in next 3 sc, (2 dc, ch 3, 2 dc) in next ch-3 sp, dc in next 3 sc, rep from * 4 times more, ch 2, sk next 2 sc, dc in next 3 sc, [2 dc, ch 3, 2 dc] in next ch-3 sp, join with sl st in top of beg ch-3.

Rnd 12: Ch 3, dc in next 2 dc, *ch 1, **puff st** (*see Special Stitch on page 128*) in next ch-2 sp, ch 1, dc in next 5 dc, (2 dc, ch 3, 2 dc) in ch-3 corner, dc in next 5 dc, rep from * to last ch-2 sp, ch 1, puff st in last ch-2 sp, ch 1, dc in next 5 dc, (2 dc, ch 3, 2 dc) in ch-3 corner, dc in last 2 dc, join with sl st in top of beg ch-3. (*42 dc, 6 puff sts*)

Fasten off.

Rnd 13: Join B with a sc in any ch-3 corner, 2 sc in same ch-3 sp, *(sc in next 7 dc, sk next ch-1 sp, sc in next puff st, sk next ch-1 sp, sc in next 7 dc), ** 3 sc in next ch-3 sp, rep from * 4 times more, rep from * to ** once, join. Fasten off. (*108 sc*)

TRIMMING ROUND
Working in unused lps on rnd 4, join C with a sc in any st, sc in each st around, join. (*24 sc*)

Join C with a sc in any sc on rnd 9, sc in each sc around, join.

Fasten off and weave in all ends.

ASSEMBLY
Referring to diagram for placement, join motifs with RS tog. Carefully matching sts, sew tog through back lps only with overcast st (*see Stitch Guide*), making sure all corner junctions are firmly joined.

BORDER
Note: For **sc dec,** *pull up lp in 2 sts indicated, yo and draw through all 3 lps on hook.*

With RS facing and short end at top, join B in 2nd sc in upper right-hand corner.

Rnd 1 (RS): 2 sc in same sc, sc in next 17 sc, 3 sc in next sc, sc in next 17 sc, **sc dec** (*see Note*) in 2nd sc of next corner and 2nd sc of corner on next motif, continue in same manner around afghan working sc in each sc, sc dec over motif joinings and 3 sc in 2nd sc of each corner, join with sl st in first sc.

Rnd 2: Ch 1, working in front lps only, sc in each sc around, join. Fasten off.

Rnd 3: Join B with sl st in first sc, ch 1, dc in each unused lp of rnd 2 around, join with sl st in beg ch-1. Fasten off.

TRIMMING ROUND
Join C with a sc in any dc, sc in each st around.

Fasten off and weave in all ends. 🦋

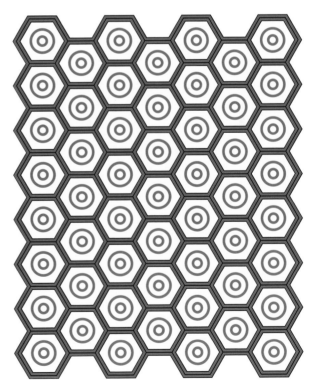

The Heat's on Hexagon Afghan

Warming Trend Versatile Afghan

DESIGN BY CINDY ADAMS

SKILL LEVEL BEGINNER

FINISHED SIZE
Approximately 40 x 54 inches

MATERIALS
 Red Heart Symphony medium (worsted) weight yarn:
    10½ oz/930 yds/294g #4907 magenta
Size J/10/6mm crochet hook or size needed to obtain gauge
Tapestry needle

GAUGE
4 shells = 5 inches

SPECIAL STITCH
Shell: In st or sp indicated work (sc, ch 3, 2 dc).

Instructions

AFGHAN CENTER
Row 1: Ch 92, sc in 2nd ch from hook and in each ch across. (*91 sc*)

Row 2: Shell (*see Special Stitch*) in first sc, sk next 2 sc, [shell in next sc, sk next 2 sc] across to last sc, sc in last sc, turn. (*30 shells*)

Row 3: Ch 1, shell in first sc, [shell in ch-3 sp of next shell] to last shell, sc in ch-3 sp of last shell, turn.

Rep row 3 until piece measures 60 inches. At end of last row, do not turn.

BORDER
Work shells evenly spaced along side of Afghan, across lower edge in unused lps of beg ch and along next side of Afghan, join with sl st in sc of first shell of last row worked.

Fasten off and weave in all ends. 🖤

Huggable Little Ones

Precious babies will be welcomed to the
world with colorful, cozy ideas just for them.

Ring-Around-Rosie Afghan & Ponchette

DESIGN BY DARLA SIMS

SKILL LEVEL ■■□□
EASY

FINISHED SIZES
Afghan: approximately 44 x 55 inches
Poncho: 9 inches long

MATERIALS

Red Heart Baby Clouds super bulky (super chunky) weight yarn:
   30 oz/740 yds/840g #9311 cloud *(A)*
   9 oz/232 yds/252g each #9363 breeze *(B)* and #9724 pink lemonade *(C)*
Size I/9/5.5mm and K/10½/6.5mm crochet hooks (for ponchette)
Size M/13/9mm crochet hook (for afghan)
Size N/13/9mm crochet hook or size needed to obtain gauge (for afghan)
Tapestry needle

GAUGE
With N hook: 2 V-sts = 3 inches

SPECIAL STITCHES
V-stitch (V-st): In st or sp indicated work (dc, ch 1, dc).

Beginning leaf (beg leaf): Ch 3 [yo twice, insert

hook in same st, yo and pull yarn through 2 lps] twice, yo and pull through all 3 lps on hook.

Leaf: [Yo twice, insert hook in next st and pull yarn through 2 lps] 3 times, yo and pull through all 4 lps on hook.

Leaf cluster (leaf cl): [Leaf, ch 2, tr, ch 2, leaf] in st or sp indicated.

Beginning popcorn (beg pc): Ch 2, 4 dc in same st, remove hook, insert hook through top of ch-2 and top lp of 4th dc, yo and pull tog.

Popcorn (pc): 5 dc in next tr, remove hook, insert hook through top lps of first and 5th dc, yo and pull tog.

Instructions

AFGHAN
With N hook and A, ch 75.

Row 1 (RS): V-st *(see Special Stitches)* in 6th ch from hook, *sk 2 chs, V-st in next ch, rep from * to last 3 chs, sk 2 chs, dc in last ch, turn. *(23 V-sts)*

Row 2: Ch 3, V-st in ch-1 sp of each V-st across, dc in last st, turn.

Rows 3–36: Rep row 2.

Fasten off and weave in all ends.

BORDER
Hold with RS facing and row 36 at top, with K hook and B, attach yarn with sl st in top lp of st in upper right-hand corner.

Rnd 1: [**Beg leaf** *(see Special Stitches)*, ch 2, tr, ch 2, **leaf** *(see Special Stitches)*] in same sp, *ch 1, tr in ch-1 sp of next V-st, ch 1, **leaf cl** *(see Special Stitches)* in ch-2 sp of next V-st*, rep from * to * 10 times more, ch 1, tr in ch-1 sp of next V-st, ch 1, leaf cl in corner dc, working along next side in ends of rows, rep from * to * to last 2 rows, ch 1, tr

CONTINUED ON PAGE 155

Watercolors Baby Set

DESIGN BY ZELDA WORKMAN

SKILL LEVEL
EASY

FINISHED SIZES
3 [6, 9] months
Instructions given fit 3 months size; changes 6 and 9 months are in [ ].

FINISHED MEASUREMENTS
Afghan: Approximately 34 x 36 inches
Hat Circumference: 16 [18, 20] inches
Poncho: 13 [14, 15] inches from shoulder to bottom center front
Poncho Rectangle: Approximately 14 x 7½ [15 x 8¾, 16 x 10] inches

MATERIALS FOR AFGHAN

Lion Brand Watercolors bulky (chunky) weight yarn:
    10½ oz/330 yds/294g #398 bright clouds *(A)*
    5¼ oz/165 yds/147g #339 sunset rose *(B)*
    1⅖ oz/45 yds/40g #347 purple haze *(C)*
    ⅘ oz/25 yds/22g #373 pond green *(D)*
Size P/15mm crochet hook or size needed to obtain gauge
Tapestry needle

GAUGE
7 sc = 4 inches; 6 rows = 4 inches

PATTERN NOTE
Afghan worked in front loops only throughout.

Instructions

AFGHAN
Row 1 (RS): With A, ch 70, sc in 2nd ch from hook and in each rem ch, turn. *(69 sc)*

Rows 2–6: Ch 1, sc in first sc, [ch 1 sk next st, sc in **front lp** *(see Stitch Guide)* of next sc] until 2 sts rem, ch 1, sk next st, sc in last sc, changing to color B, turn.

Row 7: Ch 1, sc in first sc, sc in front lp of each st until 1 st rem, sc in last sc, turn.

Row 8: Rep row 2, changing to color A, turn.

Row 9: Rep row 7.

Rows 10–12: Rep row 2, changing to color C at end of row 12.

Rows 13 & 14: Rep rows 7 and 8, changing to color A at end of row 14.

Row 15: Rep row 7, turn.

Rows 16–20: Rep row 2, changing to color D at end of row 20.

Rows 21 & 22: Rep rows 7 and 8, changing to color A at end of row 22.

Rows 23–26: Rep rows 9–12, changing to color B at end of row 26.

Rows 27 & 28: Rep rows 7 and 8, changing to color A at end of row 28.

Rows 29–34: Rep rows 15–20, changing to color C at end of row 34.

Rows 35 & 36: Rep rows 7 and 8, changing to color A at end of row 36.

Rows 37–40: Rep rows 9–12, changing to color D at end of row 40.

Rows 41 & 42: Rep rows 7 and 8, changing to color A at end of row 42.

Rows 43–48: Rep rows 15–20, changing to color B at end of row 48.

Row 49: Rep row 7.

Rows 50–52: Rep row 2. At end of row 52 do not turn.

BORDER

Rnd 1: 2 sc in last st of last row; sc in end of each row across side of Afghan, 3 sc in next corner, sc in each st across bottom, 3 sc in next corner, sc in end of each row across next side, 2 sc in same st as first sc of final row, join. Do not turn.

Rnds 2 & 3: Ch 1, [sc in each sc, 3 sc in 2nd sc of each corner] around, join. Do not turn.

Rnd 4: Ch 1, **rev sc** (*see Stitch Guide*) in each sc around, join.

Fasten off and weave in all ends.

Hat

MATERIALS FOR HAT

Lion Brand Watercolors bulky (chunky) weight yarn:
1 oz/30 yds/26.6g #398 bright clouds *(A)*
³⁄₂₀ oz/5 yds/4.5g #339 sunset rose *(B)*
³⁄₁₀ oz/10 yds/9g [½ oz/15 yds/13.4g,
⅔ oz/20 yds/18g] #347 purple haze *(C)*
³⁄₁₀ oz/10 yds/9g [³⁄₁₀ oz/10 yds/9g,
½ oz/15 yds/13.4g] #373 pond green *(D)*
Size P/15mm crochet hook or size needed
to obtain gauge

HAT

Size 3 Months Only

Rnd 1: With A, ch 2, 9 sc in 2nd ch from hook, join with sl st to top of first sc. (*9 sc*)

Rnd 2: Working in **front lps** (*see Stitch Guide*) only now and throughout, ch 1, 2 sc in each sc, changing to D in last st, join. (*18 sc*)

Rnd 3: Ch 1, [sc in next 5 sc, 2 sc in next sc] around, changing to A in last st, join. (*21 sc*)

Rnd 4: Ch 1, [sc in next 6 sc, 2 sc in next sc] around, join. (*24 sc*)

Rnd 5: Ch 1, [sc in next 7 sc, 2 sc in next sc] around, changing to B in last st, join. (*27 sc*)

Rnd 6: Ch 1, [sc in next 8 sc, 2 sc in next sc] around, changing to A in last st, join. (*30 sc*)

Rnd 7: Ch 1, sc in each sc around, join.

Rnd 8: Ch 1, sc in each sc around, changing to C in last st, join.

Rnd 9: Ch 1, sc in each sc around, join.

Rnd 10: Ch 1, **rev sc** (*see Stitch Guide*) in each sc around, join.

Fasten off and weave in all ends.

Size 6 Months Only

Rnd 1: With A, ch 2, 11 sc in 2nd ch from hook, join with sl st to top of first sc. (*11 sc*)

Rnd 2: Working in **front lps** (*see Stitch Guide*) only now and throughout, ch 1, 2 sc in each sc, changing to D in last st, join. (*22 sc*)

Rnd 3: Ch 1, [sc in next 6 sc, 2 sc in next sc] 3 times, sc in last sc, changing to A in last st, join. (*25 sc*)

Rnd 4: Ch 1, [sc in next 7 sc, 2 sc in next sc] 3 times, sc in last sc, join. (*28 sc*)

Rnd 5: Ch 1, [sc in next 8 sc, 2 sc in next sc] 3 times, sc in last sc, changing to B in last st, join. (*31 sc*)

Rnd 6: Ch 1, [sc in next 9 sc, 2 sc in next sc] 3 times, sc in last sc, changing to A in last st, join. (*34 sc*)

Rnd 7: Ch 1, sc in each sc around, join.

Rnd 8: Ch 1, sc in each sc around, changing to C in last st, join.

Rnds 9 & 10: Ch 1, sc in each sc around, join.

Rnd 11: Ch 1, **rev sc** (*see Stitch Guide*) in each sc around, join.

Fasten off and weave in all ends.

Size 9 Months Only

Rnd 1: With A, ch 2, 12 sc in 2nd ch from hook, join with sl st to top of first sc. (*12 sc*)

Rnd 2: Working in **front lps** *(see Stitch Guide)* only now and throughout, ch 1, 2 sc in each sc, changing to D in last st, join. *(24 sc)*

Rnd 3: Ch 1, [sc in next 11 sc, 2 sc in next sc] around, join. *(26 sc)*

Rnd 4: Ch 1, [sc in next 12 sc, 2 sc in next sc] around, changing to A in last st, join. *(28 sc)*

Rnd 5: Ch 1, [sc in next 13 sc, 2 sc in next sc] around, join. *(30 sc)*

Rnd 6: Ch 1, [sc in next 14 sc, 2 sc in next sc] around, changing to B in last st, join. *(32 sc)*

Rnd 7: Ch 1, [sc in next 15 sc, 2 sc in next sc] around, join. *(34 sc)*

Rnd 8: Ch 1, [sc in next 7 sc, 2 sc in next sc, sc in next 8 sc, 2 sc in next sc] around, changing to A in last st, join. *(38 sc)*

Rnds 9 & 10: Ch 1, sc in each sc around, changing to C in last st, join.

Rnd 11: Ch 1, sc in each sc around, join.

Rnd 12: Ch 1, **rev sc** *(see Stitch Guide)* in each sc around, join.

Fasten off and weave in all ends.

Poncho

MATERIALS FOR PONCHO

 Lion Brand Watercolors bulky (chunky) weight yarn:
    1¾ oz/55 yds/49g #398 bright clouds *(A)*
    1¹⁄₁₀ oz/35 yds/31g #339 sunset rose *(B)*
    1⁴⁄₁₀ oz/45 yds/40g [1¾ oz/55 yds/4g,
    1¾ oz/55 yds/49g] #347 purple haze *(C)*
    ³⁄₁₀ oz/10 yds/9g [³⁄₁₀ oz/10 yds/9g,
    ½ oz/15 yds/13.4g] #373 pond green *(D)*
Size P/15mm crochet hook or size needed
    to obtain gauge
Tapestry needle
3 buttons to match color C, ⅞-inch-diameter
Sewing needle and matching thread

PATTERN NOTE
Poncho is worked in front loops only throughout.

PONCHO

Size 3 Months Only
RECTANGLE 1
Row 1: With C, ch 26, sc in 2nd ch from hook and in each ch across, changing to A in last st, turn. *(25 sc)*

Row 2: Ch 1, sc in each st across, turn.

Row 3: Ch 1, sc in first sc, [ch 1, sk next sc, sc in next sc] across, changing to B in last st, turn.

Row 4: Ch 1, sc in each st and in each ch-1 sp across, changing to A in last st, turn.

Row 5: Ch 1, sc in each st across, turn.

Row 6: Ch 1, sc in first sc, [ch 1, sk next sc, sc in next sc] across, changing to D in last st, turn.

Row 7: Ch 1, sc in each st across, changing to A in last st, turn.

Row 8: Rep row 5.

Row 9: Ch 1, sc in first sc, [ch 1, sk next sc, sc in next sc] across, changing to C in last st, turn.

Row 10: Ch 1, sc in each st across, turn.

BORDER
Ch 1, working through both lps, 3 sc in first sc, sc in each st across to last st, 3 sc in last st; working across next side, sc in end of each row to corner, 3 sc in first st of foundation ch, sc in each st to last st, 3 sc in last sc; working across next side, sc in end of each row to first sc, join.

Fasten off and weave in all ends.

RECTANGLE 2
Work same as for Rectangle 1. At end of border, do not fasten off, turn.

BUTTONHOLE FLAP
Row 1: Ch 1, sc in each sc to first sc of next corner, turn.

Row 2: Ch 1, sc in first 2 sc, [ch 1, sk next sc, sc in next 3 sc] twice, sc across, turn.

Row 3: Ch 1, sc in each st across.

Fasten off and weave in all ends.

Continue with Finishing.

Size 6 Months Only
RECTANGLE 1
Row 1: With C, ch 28, sc in 2nd ch from hook and in each ch across, turn. (*27 sc*)

Row 2: Ch 1, sc in first sc, [ch 1, sk next sc, sc in next sc] across, changing to A in last st, turn.

Row 3: Ch 1, sc in each st and ch-1 sp across, turn.

Row 4: Ch 1, sc in first sc, [ch 1, sk next sc, sc in next sc] across, changing to B in last st, turn.

Row 5: Ch 1, sc in each st and in each ch-1 sp across, changing to A in last st, turn.

Row 6: Ch 1, sc in each st across, turn.

Row 7: Ch 1, sc in first sc, [ch 1, sk next sc, sc in next sc] across, changing to D in last st, turn.

Row 8: Ch 1, sc in each st and in each ch-1 sp across, changing to A in last st, turn.

Row 9: Rep row 6.

Row 10: Ch 1, sc in first sc, [ch 1, sk next sc, sc in next sc] across, changing to C in last st, turn.

Rows 11 & 12: Ch 1, sc in each st across, turn.

BORDER
Ch 1, working through both lps, 3 sc in first sc, sc in each st across to last st, 3 sc in last st; working across next side, sc in end of each row to corner, 3 sc in first st of foundation ch, sc in each st to last st, 3 sc in last sc; working across next side, sc in end of each row to first sc, join.

Fasten off and weave in all ends.

RECTANGLE 2
Work same as for Rectangle 1. At end of border, do not fasten off, turn.

BUTTONHOLE FLAP
Row 1: Ch 1, sc in each sc to first sc of next corner, turn.

Row 2: Ch 1, sc in first 2 sc, [ch 1, sk next sc, sc in next 3 sc] twice, sc across, turn.

Row 3: Ch 1, sc in each st across.

Fasten off and weave in all ends.

Continue with Finishing.

For Size 9 Months Only
RECTANGLE 1
Row 1: With C, ch 30, sc in 2nd ch from hook and in each ch across, turn. (*29 sc*)

Row 2: Ch 1, sc in first sc, [ch 1, sk next sc, sc in next sc] across, changing to A in last st, turn.

Row 3: Ch 1, sc in each st and ch-1 sp across, turn.

Row 4: Ch 1, sc in first sc, [ch 1, sk next sc, sc in next sc] across, changing to B in last st, turn.

Row 5: Ch 1, sc in each st and ch-1 sp across, changing to A in last st, turn.

Row 6: Ch 1, sc in first sc, [ch 1, sk next sc, sc in next sc] across, changing to A in last st, turn.

Row 7: Ch 1, sc in each st and ch-1 sp across, turn.

Row 8: Ch 1, sc in first sc, [ch 1, sk next sc, sc in next sc] across, changing to D in last st, turn.

Row 9: Ch 1, sc in each st and in each ch-1 sp across, changing to A in last st, turn.

Row 10: Ch 1, sc in first sc, [ch 1, sk next sc, sc in next sc] across, changing to A in last st, turn.

Row 11: Rep row 7.

Row 12: Ch 1, sc in first sc, [ch 1, sk next sc, sc in next sc] across, changing to C in last st, turn.

Rows 13 & 14: Ch 1, sc in each st across, turn.

BORDER
Ch 1, working through both lps, 3 sc in first sc, sc in each st across to last st, 3 sc in last st; working across next side, sc in end of each row to corner, 3 sc in first st of foundation ch, sc in each st to last st, 3 sc in last sc; working across next side, sc in end of each row to first sc, join.

Fasten off and weave in all ends.

RECTANGLE 2
Work same as for Rectangle 1. At end of border, do not fasten off, turn.

BUTTONHOLE FLAP
Row 1: Ch 1, sc in each sc to first sc of next corner, turn.

Row 2: Ch 1, sc in first 2 sc, [ch 1, sk next sc, sc in next 3 sc] twice, sc across, turn.

Row 3: Ch 1, sc in each st across.

Fasten off and weave in all ends.

FINISHING
With C, join edges as shown in Fig. 1. Mark for placement and sew buttons to Rectangle 1 using sewing thread. Use sewing thread to tighten edges of buttonholes as needed.

EDGING
Join C in any edge st, ch 1, **rev sc** *(see Stitch Guide)* in each st around, join.

Fasten off and weave in all ends. ❦

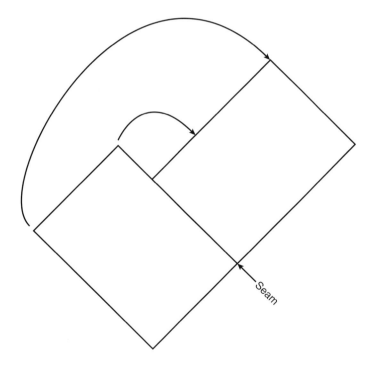

Fig. 1

Little Princess Baby Sweater

DESIGN BY DIANE SIMPSON

SKILL LEVEL ◼◼◻◻
EASY

FINISHED SIZES
Instructions given fit 6–9 months; changes for 9–12 months and 12–18 months are in [ ].

FINISHED GARMENT MEASUREMENTS
Chest: 21½ [22¼, 23] inches

MATERIALS
 Patons Katrina medium (worsted) weight yarn: 10 oz/466 yds/280g [13 oz/605 yds/364g, 16 oz/745 yds/448g] #10732 blossom (A)
 Bernat Boa bulky (chunky) weight yarn: 1¾ oz/71 yds/49g for all #81005 dove (B)
Size I/9/5.5mm crochet hook or size needed to obtain gauge
Size M/13/9mm crochet hook
5 novelty buttons, ½-inch diameter
Tapestry needle
Sewing needle and thread to match yarn

GAUGE
With smaller hook and A: 16 sc = 4 inches; 16 sc rows = 4 inches

PATTERN NOTES
Except for turning chain-1, all chains and stitches count as a stitch.
Bodice is worked in one piece to underarm.

Instructions

SWEATER
RIBBING
With smaller hook and A, ch 5.

Row 1: Sc in 2nd ch from hook, sc in each ch across, turn. *(4 sc)*

Rows 2–76 [80, 84]: Ch 1, working in **back lps** *(see Stitch Guide)* only, sc in each st across, turn. Do not fasten off.

BODICE
Note: *For **dec,** draw up lp in each of 2 sts indicated, yo and draw through all 3 lps on hook.*

Row 1 (RS): Ch 1, sc in end of each row of ribbing across, turn. *(76 [80, 84] sts)*

Row 2: Ch 1, sc in first st, [ch 1, sk next st, sc in next st] across to last st, sc in last st, turn.

Rows 3–8 [10, 12]: Ch 1, sc in first st, [ch 1, sk next st, sc in next ch-1 sp] across to last st, sc in last st, turn.

Row 9 [11, 13]: For right front, ch 1, sc in first st, [ch 1, sk next st, sc in next ch-1 sp] 9 [9, 10] times, turn leaving rem sts unworked. *(19, [19, 21] sts)*

Row 10 [12, 14]: For right sleeve, ch 22 [26, 30], sc in 2nd ch from hook, [ch 1, sk next ch, sc in next st] across ch, [ch 1, sk next st, sc in next ch-1 sp] across previous row, turn. *(40 [44, 50] sts)*

Rows 11–19 [13–23, 15–27]: Rep row 3.

Row 20 [24, 28]: Ch 1, sc in first st, [ch 1, sk next st, sc in next ch-1 sp] 15 [16, 18] times, ch 1, sk next st, **dec** *(see Note)* in next ch-1 sp and next st, turn leaving rem sts unworked for neck shaping. *(33 [35, 39] sts)*

Row 21 [25, 29]: Ch 1, dec in first sc and ch-1 sp, [ch 1, sk next st, sc in next ch-1 sp] across, turn. *(32 [34, 38] sts)*

Rows 22–27 [26–31, 30–35]: Rep row 3. At end of last row, fasten off.

BACK
Row 1 (RS): Hold with RS facing, ch 21 [25, 29], sc in first unworked st of row 8 [10, 12] on Bodice, sc in next ch-1 sp [ch 1, sk next st, sc in next ch-1 sp] 18 [20, 20] times, turn. *(38 [42, 42] sts plus beg chs)*

Row 2: Ch 22 [26, 30], sc in 2nd ch from hook, [ch 1, sk next ch, sc in next ch] across chs, ch 1, [sk next st, sc in next ch-1 sp, ch 1] across previous row to first ch of beg ch, [sc in next ch, ch 1, sk next ch] across to last ch, sc in last ch, turn. *[80 (92, 100) sts]*

Rows 3–17 [17, 19]: Ch 1, sc in first st, [ch 1, sk next st, sc in next ch-1 sp] across to last st, sc in last st, turn.

At end of last row, fasten off.

LEFT FRONT

Row 1 (RS): Hold with RS facing, ch 21 [25, 29], sc first unworked st of row 8 [10, 12] on bodice, work in pat across, turn. *(19 [19, 21] sts plus beg chs)*

Row 2: Work in pat across previous row and added chs. *(40 [44, 50] sts)*

Rows 3–11 [11, 13]: Work in pat across.

Row 12 [12, 14]: Ch 1, sl st in first 6 (8, 10) sts and sps for neck shaping, ch 1, dec in next ch-1 sp and next st, [ch 1, sk next st, sc in next ch-1 sp] across, turn. *(33 [35, 39] sts)*

Row 13 [13, 15]: Ch 1, sc in first st, [ch 1, sk next ch, sc in next ch-1 sp] across to last ch-1 sp and st, dec in last 2 sts, turn. *(32 [34, 38] sts)*

Rows 14–19 [14–19, 16–21]: Rep row 3. At end of last row, fasten off.

PEPLUM

Row 1: With WS facing of ribbing at top, working on opposite side of waist ribbing, join with sl st in end of row in upper right-hand corner, ch 3, 2 dc in end of each row across, turn. *(151 [159, 167] sts)*

Row 2 (RS): Ch 1, sc in first st, [ch 1, sk next st, sc in next st] across, turn.

Rows 3–6 [7, 8]: Ch 1, sc in first st, [ch 1, sk next st, sc in next st] across, turn. At end of last row, fasten off.

ASSEMBLY

Sew shoulder and underarm sleeve seams.

BUTTONHOLE PLACKET

Note: *Work rem rows in back lps only unless otherwise stated.*

Row 1: Hold with RS of right front facing, with smaller hook, join A with sl st in end of last row on Peplum, ch 5, sc in 2nd ch from hook, sc in each ch across, sl st in end of next row, turn. *(4 sc)*

Row 2: Ch 1, sc in each st across, turn.

Row 3: Ch 1, sc in each st across, sl st in end of next row, turn.

Rows 4–9 [11, 11]: Rep rows 2 and 3.

Row 10 [12, 12]: For *buttonhole row,* sc in first st, ch 1, sk next st, sc in last 2 sts, turn.

Row 11 [13, 13]: Rep row 3.

Rows 12–15 [14–17, 14–17]: Rep rows 2 and 3.

Row 16 [18, 18]: Rep row 10 [12, 12].

Rows 17–28 [19–30, 19–30]: Rep rows 11–16 [13–18, 13–18] twice.

Rows 29–31 [31–33, 31–35]: Rep rows 11–13 [13–15, 13–17].

BUTTON PLACKET

Note: *Work rem rows in back lps only unless otherwise stated.*

Row 1: Hold with WS of left front facing, with smaller hook, join A with sl st in end of last row on Peplum, ch 5, sc in 2nd ch from hook, sc in each ch across, sl st in end of next row, turn. *(4 sc)*

Row 2: Ch 1, sc in each st across, turn.

Row 3: Ch 1, sc in each st across, sl st in end of next row, turn.

Rows 4–31 [33, 35]: Rep rows 2 and 3. At end of last row, fasten off and weave in all ends.

TRIM
LOWER EDGE

Hold with WS of lower edge at top, with larger hook and B, join with sl st in first st of Buttonhole Placket, ch 2, hdc in each st across lower edge. Fasten off.

SLEEVE

Hold one sleeve with WS facing, join with sl st in underarm seam, ch 2, hdc in each st around, join in top of beg ch-2. Fasten off.

Rep on other sleeve.

NECK

Hold with WS facing and neck edge at top, ch 2, hdc evenly spaced around neck edge. Fasten off.

FINISHING

Sew buttons opposite buttonholes on Buttonhole Placket. Sew rem button at top on neck trim using sp between sts for buttonhole.

Ring-Around-Rosie Afghan & Ponchette CONTINUED FROM PAGE 144

in next row, ch 1, leaf cl in corner, work rem 2 sides in similar manner having same number of leaf cls as on opposite side; join with sl st in top of beg ch-3. Fasten off.

Row 2: Attach C with sl st to corner tr, **beg pc** (see Special Stitches) in same st, [ch 4, **pc** (see Special Stitches) in next tr] around, join with sl st in top of first pc.

Fasten off and weave in all ends.

PONCHETTE

With I hook and A, ch 33, join to form a ring.

Rnd 1: [Ch 4, (counts as dc and ch-1 sp) dc] in same sp (beg V-st), *sk 2 chs, **V-st** (see Special Stitches) in next ch, rep from * around; join with sl st in 3rd ch of beg ch-4. (11 V-sts)

Change to K hook.

Rnd 2: Sl st in center of first V-st, (beg V-st, V-st) in same sp, 2 V-sts in ch-1 sp of each V-st around, join in top of beg ch-3. (22 V-sts)

Rnd 3: Sl st in center of first V-st, (beg V-st, V-st) in same sp, V-st in each V-st around, join. (22 V-sts)

Change to M hook.

Rnds 4–6: Sl st in center of first V-st, (beg V-st, V-st) in same sp, work V-st in each V-st around, join.

BORDER

Rnd 1: With M hook, attach B with sl st in ch-1 sp of any V-st, **beg leaf** (see Special Stitches on page 144), ch 2, tr, ch 2, **leaf** (see Special Stitches)] in same sp, ch 2, tr in ch-1 sp of next V-st, *leaf cl (see Special Stitches) in next V-st, ch 2, tr in next V-st, ch 2], rep from * around, join in top of beg ch-3. Fasten off.

Rnd 2: Attach C with sl st in any tr, work **beg pc** (see Special Stitches) in same st, [ch 5, **pc** (see Special Stitches) in next tr] around, join to top of beg pc.

Fasten off and weave in all ends.

Little Miss Hat

DESIGN BY JOY PRESCOTT

SKILL LEVEL
EASY

FINISHED SIZES
Instructions given fit infant; changes for toddler and child are in [ ].

FINISHED MEASUREMENTS
Head circumference: 14 [16, 18] inches

MATERIALS
 Bernat Baby Coordinates light (light worsted) weight yarn:
⁹⁄₁₀ oz/70 yds/25g [1¹⁄₁₀ oz/85 yds/30g, 1¼ oz/100 yds/36g] #01001 pink *(A)*
 Lion Brand Fun Fur bulky (chunky) weight eyelash yarn:
²⁄₅ oz/13 yds/10.6g [²⁄₅ oz/14 yds/11.5g, ½ oz/15 yds/12.3g] #100 white *(B)*
Size H/8/5mm crochet hook or size needed to obtain gauge
Tapestry needle

GAUGE
First 4 rnds (dc) = 2 inches; 9 dc = 2 inches

PATTERN NOTE
Join with slip stitch unless otherwise stated.

SPECIAL STITCHES
Wattle stitch (wattle st): [Sc, ch 1, dc] in same sp.

Puff stitch (puff st): 3 dc in same st, drop lp from hook, insert hook into first dc, pick up lp and pull through st, ch 1.

Instructions

HAT
For Infant Hat Only
With A, ch 4.

Rnd 1: 11 dc in 4th ch from hook *(beg 3 sk chs count as a dc)*, join in top of beg 3 sk chs. *(12 sts)*

Rnd 2: Ch 3 *(counts as first dc now and through-out)*, dc in same st, 2 dc in each st around, join in top of ch-3. *(24 sts)*

Rnd 3: Ch 3, [2 dc in next st, dc in next st] around, join. *(36 sts)*

Rnd 4: Ch 3, dc in next st [2 dc in next st, dc in each of next 2 sts] around, join. *(48 sts)*

Rnd 5: [**Wattle st** *(see Special Stitches)* in first st, sk next 2 sts] around, join in first sc. *(16 wattle sts)*

Rnd 6: Ch 1, wattle st in each ch-1 sp around, join with sl st in first sc.

Rnd 7: Ch 1, [wattle st in each of next 3 ch-1 sps, 2 wattle sts in next ch-1 sp] around, join in first sc. *(20 wattle sts)*

Rnds 8–16: Ch 1, wattle st in each ch-1 sp around, join in first sc.

Rnd 17: Ch 1, [wattle st in each of next 2 ch-1 sps, 2 wattle sts in next ch-1 sp] to last 2 wattle sts, wattle st in each of next 2 ch-1 sps, join in first sc. Fasten off. *(26 wattle sts)*

Rnd 18: Join B with sl st in any ch-1 sp, ch 1, sc in same sp, sc in each st around, join in first sc. *(78 sts)*

Fasten off and weave in all ends.

For Toddler Hat Only
With A, ch 4.

Rnds 1–8: Rep rnds 1–8 of Infant Hat.

Rnd 9: Ch 1, [wattle st in each of next 4 ch-1 sps, 2 wattle sts in next ch-1 sp] around, join in first sc. *(24 wattle sts)*

Rnds 10–18: Ch 1, wattle st in each ch-1 sp around, join in first sc.

Rnd 19: Ch 1, [wattle st in each of next 3 ch-1 sps, 2 wattle sts in next ch-1 sp] around, join in first sc. *(30 wattle sts)*

Fasten off.

Rnd 20: Join B with sl st in any ch-1 sp, ch 1, sc in same sp, sc in each st around, join in first sc. *(90 sts)*

Fasten off and weave in all ends.

CONTINUED ON PAGE 161

Soft-as-Snow Toddler Jacket

DESIGN BY DARLA SIMS

SKILL LEVEL ◼◼◻◻
EASY

FINISHED SIZES
Instructions given fit 1 year; changes for 2 years and 4 years are in [ ].

FINISHED MEASUREMENTS
Chest: 22 [24, 26] inches

MATERIALS

Moda Dea Dream medium (worsted) weight yarn:
8²⁄₅ oz/465 yds/247g [10½ oz/558 yds/294g, 12³⁄₁₀ oz/651 yds/344g] #3101 winter white *(A)*
Red Heart Foxy bulky (chunky) weight yarn:
1¾ oz/89 yds/50g [1¾ oz/89 yds/50g, 1¾ oz/89 yds/50g] #9251 cherries *(B)*
Red Heart Classic medium (worsted) weight yarn:
3½ oz/198 yds/98g #730 grenadine *(C)*
Size G/6/4mm, H/8/5mm, I/9/5.5mm crochet hooks or sizes needed to obtain gauge
Tapestry needle
Stitch markers

GAUGE
Using I hook: 3 sts = 1 inch
Take time to check gauge.

SPECIAL STITCH
Pattern Stitch (pat st): Dc in next st, sc in next st.

Instructions

JACKET
BODY
With I hook and A, ch 73 [79, 83].

Row 1 (RS): Sc in 2nd ch from hook, [dc in next ch, sc in next ch] across to last ch, dc in last ch, turn. *(72 [78, 82] sts)*

Row 2: Ch 1, sc in first st, work pat st across, dc in last st, turn.

Rep row 2 until piece measures 7½ [9, 10] inches in length, ending with a RS row.

RIGHT FRONT
Row 1: Ch 1, work pat st across next 19 [21, 22] sts, turn. *(19 [21, 22] sts)*

Rep row 1 until piece measures 9 [11½, 13½] inches long, ending with a WS row. Cut yarn.

SHAPE NECK
Note: *For dec, [yo, pull up lp in next st] twice, yo and draw through all 3 lps on hook.*

Row 1: Sk first 8 sts, sl st in next st, ch 1, sc in same st, work pat st across, turn. *(11 [13, 14] sts)*

Row 2: Ch 1, work pat st across, turn.

Row 3: Ch 1, [**dec** *(see Note)* in next 2 sts] work in pat st across, turn. *(10 [12, 13] sts)*

Row 4: Ch 1, work in pat st across, turn.

For 1 Year Size Only
Rows 5–7: Rep row 4. Fasten off. *(10 sts)*

For 2 Years & 4 Years Sizes Only
Rows 5 & 6: Rep rows 3 and 4. *(11 [12] sts)*

Row 7: Rep row 4. Fasten off.

LEFT FRONT
Row 1 (RS): With RS facing, sk next 34 [36, 38] sts for center back, attach yarn in next st, ch 3 *(counts as dc)*, work in pat st across. *(19 [21, 22] sts)*

Row 2: Ch 1, work in pat st across, turn.

Rep row 2 until piece measures 9 [11½, 13½] inches in length, ending with a WS row. Cut yarn.

SHAPE NECK
Row 1 (RS): Join with sl st in first st, work in pat st across, leaving last 8 sts unworked, turn. *(11 [13, 14] st)*

Rows 2: Ch 1, work in pat st across, turn.

Rows 3: Ch 1, work in pat st to last 2 sts, dec in next 2 sts, turn. *(10 [12, 13] sts)*

Row 4: Ch 1, work in pat st across, turn.

For 1 Year Size Only
Rows 5–7: Rep row 4. Fasten off. *(10 sts)*

For 2 Years & 4 Years Sizes Only
Rows 5 & 6: Rep rows 3 and 4. *(11 [12] sts)*

Row 7: Rep row 4. Fasten off.

BACK
Row 1(RS): With RS facing, attach yarn in next st after Right Front, ch 3 *(counts as a dc)*, work in pat st as established across. *(34 [36, 38] sts)*

Row 2: Ch 1, work in pat st across, turn.

Rep row 2 until Back is same length as Fronts.

Fasten off.

SLEEVES
With I hook and A, ch 19 [21, 25].

Row 1: Sc in 2nd ch from hook, [dc in next ch, sc in next ch] across, dc in last ch, turn. *(18 [20, 24] sts)*

Row 2: Ch 1, sc in first st, pat st across, dc in last st, turn.

Row 3: Ch 1, 2 sc *(inc)* in first st, pat st across to last st, 2 dc in last st *(inc)*, turn.

Row 4: Ch 1, sc in first 2 sts, pat st to last 2 sts, dc in next 2 sts, turn.

Row 5: Ch 1, 2 sc in first st *(inc)*, sc in next st, pat st to last 2 sts, dc in next st, 2 dc in last st *(inc)*, turn.

Row 6: Ch 1, sc in first st, pat st to last st, dc in last st, turn.

Rows 7–10: Rep rows 3–6. *(26 [28, 32] sts)*

Rows 11 & 12: Rep rows 3 and 4. *(28 [30, 34] sts)*

Rep row 4, until Sleeve length measures 7 [9, 10½] inches. Fasten off.

ASSEMBLY
Sew shoulder seams. Sew Sleeve seams and set in Sleeves. Place markers for 3 Flowers, evenly spaced on Right Front.

EDGINGS
BODY EDGING
Rnd 1: Hold with RS facing and neck edge at top, With H hook and A, attach yarn to neck edge of Right Front, ch 1 and 3 sc in same st, work 13 sc to shoulder seam, work 14 [14, 16] sts across back neck, work 13 sc from shoulder seam to center front, work 3 sc in corner, work in sc around Body to first marker on Right Front, ch 7 for button lp, sl st in last st, [sc to next marker, ch 7 for button lp, sl st in last st] twice, join.

Rnd 2: Ch 1, sc around neck edge only to center sc of Left Front corner. Fasten off.

LOWER EDGING
Row 1: Hold with RS facing and lower edge at top, with H hook attach B in first sc in upper right-hand corner, ch 2, hdc in each sc across, turn.

Row 2: Ch 2, hdc across. Fasten off.

SLEEVE EDGING
Rnd 1: With H hook and A, attach in one Sleeve seam, ch 1, sc in same st and in each st around, join in first sc, changing to B.

Rnds 2: Ch 2, hdc around, join.

Rnd 3: Rep rnd 2. Fasten off.

HOOD
Row 1: With I hook and A, ch 17 [19, 21], sc in 2nd ch from hook [dc in next st, sc in next st] across, dc in last ch, turn. *(16 [18, 20] sts)*

Row 2: Ch 1, sc in first st, pat st across to last st, dc in last st, turn.

Rep row 2 until piece measures 14 [16, 18] inches long, ending with a RS row. Fold in half and sew one side for back seam.

HOOD EDGING
With H hook attach A to seam, ch 1 and sc in same st, sc around Hood, join. Fasten off.

FRONT EDGING
Row 1: Hold Hood with RS facing and long open edge at top, with H hook, attach B in right-hand corner of Hood, ch 2, hdc around long edge, turn.

Row 2: Ch 2, hdc in each hdc across.

Fasten off and weave in all ends.

Sew Hood around neck.

FLOWERS
Make 6.
Rnd 1: With G hook and C, ch 2, 9 sc in 2nd ch from hook. Do not turn.

Rnd 2: Sl st in first st, [ch 2, sl st in 2nd ch from hook, sl st in next st] around. Fasten off.

CENTER
Make 6.
With G hook and A, ch 4, 4 dc in 4th ch from hook, remove hook, insert hook through 3rd ch of beg ch and top lp of last dc, yo and pull tog.

Pull through center of Flower and sew to back of Flower.

Sew 3 Flowers to Left Front opposite buttonholes. Sew rem Flowers to Right Front beside buttonholes. 💕

Little Miss Hat CONTINUED FROM PAGE 156

For Child Hat Only
With A, ch 4.

Rnds 1–10: Rep rnds 1–10 of Toddler Hat.

Rnd 11: Ch 1, [wattle st in each of next 5 ch-1 sps, 2 wattle sts in next ch-1 sp] around, join in first sc. *(28 wattle sts)*

Rnds 12–20: Ch 1, wattle st in each ch-1 sp around, join in first sc.

Rnd 21: Ch 1, [wattle st in each of next 3 ch-1 sps, 2 wattle sts in next ch-1 sp] around, join in first sc. *(35 wattle sts)*

Fasten off.

Rnd 22: Join B with sl st in any ch-1 sp, ch 1, sc in same sp, sc in each st around, join with sl st in first sc. *(105 sts)*

Fasten off and weave in all ends.

FLOWER
With A, ch 4.

Rnd 1: Work 7 **puff sts** *(see Special Stitches)* in 4th ch from hook, join in first puff st. Fasten off.

Rnd 2: Join B with sl st in any ch-1 sp, ch 1, sc in same sp as joining, [ch 6, dc in 4th ch from hook, dc in next 2 chs, sc in next ch-1 sp (petal)] around, join in first st. *(7 petals)*

Fasten off and weave in all ends.

FINISHING
Fold last 3 rnds up to form brim of Hat. Using tapestry needle, sew Flower to front of Hat. 💕

Mint Cozy Grannies Baby Afghan

DESIGN BY CINDY ADAMS

SKILL LEVEL EASY

FINISHED SIZE
Approximately 36 x 44 inches.

MATERIALS
  Bernat Baby Lash bulky (chunky) weight yarn:
8¾ oz/250 yds/245g #67230 gentle green (A)
Bernat Satin medium (worsted) weight yarn:
17½ oz/315 yds/490g #04230 spring (B)
Size J/10/6mm crochet hook or size needed to
obtain gauge
Tapestry needle

GAUGE
Square = 7¼ inches

Instructions

SQUARE
Make 30.
Rnd 1 (RS): With A, ch 6, join to form a ring, ch 3 (counts as a dc on this and following rnds), 15 dc in ring, join with sl st in top of beg ch-3. (16 dc)

Rnd 2: Sl st between ch-3 and next dc, ch 5 (counts as a dc and ch-2 sp), [dc between next 2 dc, ch 2] 15 times, join with sl st in 3rd ch of beg ch-5. Fasten off.

Rnd 3: Join B in any ch-2 sp, ch 3, 2 dc in same sp, ch 1, [3 dc in next ch-2 sp, ch 1] 15 times, join with sl st in top of beg ch-3. (48 dc)

Rnd 4: Sl st in next 2 dc and in next ch-1 sp, *ch 5 (corner), sc in next ch-1 sp, [ch 3, sc in next ch-1 sp] 3 times, rep from * twice more, ch 5 (corner), sc in next ch-1 sp, [ch 3, sc in next ch-1 sp] twice, ch 3, join in first ch of beg ch-5.

Rnd 5: Sl st in same ch-5 sp, (ch 3, 2 dc, ch 2, 3 dc) in same sp (beg corner); 3 dc in each of next 3 ch-3 sp, *(3 dc, ch 2, 3 dc) in next ch-5 sp (corner), 3 dc in each of next 3 ch-3 sp, rep from * twice more, join in top of beg ch-3. (60 dc)

Fasten off and weave in all ends.

JOINING SQUARES
Hold 2 Squares with RS tog, sl st through outside lps.

Join rem Squares in similar manner, working 6 rows with 5 Squares in each row. Sl st the rows tog in similar manner making sure all 4-corner joinings are secure.

BORDER
Hold Afghan with RS facing and one short edge at top, join B with a sc in st after corner ch-2 sp in upper right-hand corner, *[sc in each st, 2 sc in each corner] to next outer corner ch-2 sp, 3 sc in corner ch-2 sp, rep from * 3 times; join in joining sc.

Fasten off and weave in all ends. ❧

So-Soft High-Five Baby Afghan

DESIGN BY CINDY ADAMS

SKILL LEVEL
EASY

FINISHED SIZE
Approximately 36 x 46 inches.

MATERIALS

- Bernat LuLu medium (worsted) weight yarn:
3½ oz/272 yds/98g each #36510 peachy keen
(A), #36615 yoyo yellow *(B)* and #36742
silly sky *(C)*
- Size I/9/5.5mm crochet hook or size needed to
obtain gauge

GAUGE
10 dc = 5 inches

SPECIAL STITCH
Front post triple crochet (fptr): Yo twice, insert
hook from front to back around **post** *(see Stitch
Guide)* of st indicated, draw up lp, [yo, draw
through 2 lps on hook] 3 times. **Note:** *Sk st behind
fptr on working row.*

COLOR SEQUENCE
2 rows each A, B, C in sequence.

Instructions

AFGHAN
With A, ch 76.

Row 1 (RS): Dc in 3rd ch from hook *(2 sk chs count
as a dc)* and in each rem ch, turn. *(75 dc)*

Row 2: Ch 2 *(counts as first dc now and throughout)*, dc in each dc to beg 2 sk chs, dc in 2nd ch of
beg 2 sk chs, changing to B in last st, turn.

Row 3: Ch 2, dc in next 4 dc *fptr *(see Special
Stitch)* around each of next 5 dc on 2nd row

below, on working row, dc in next 15 dc, rep from
* to last 10 sts, fptr around each of next 5 dc on
2nd row below, dc in last 4 dc and in 2nd ch of
turning ch-2, turn.

Row 4: Ch 2, dc in each st to turning ch-2, dc in 2nd
ch of turning ch-2, changing to C in last st, turn.

Row 5: Ch 2, dc in next 14 dc, *fptr around each of
next 5 dc on 2nd row below, on working row, dc in
next 15 dc, rep from * across, turn.

Row 6: Rep row 4.

Working in Color Sequence, rep rows 3–6 for
desired length, ending with 2 rows of A.

Fasten off and weave in all ends.

Fuzzy Baby Slippers

DESIGN BY KATHLEEN STUART

SKILL LEVEL
EASY

SIZES
Instructions given fit up to 4¼-inch sole.

MATERIALS
 Lion Brand Polarspun bulky (chunky) weight yarn:
  1¾ oz/137 yds/49g #245 tutti fruity *or* #201 candy pink *or* #205 delft
Size J/10/6mm crochet hook *or* size needed to obtain gauge
Tapestry needle

GAUGE
4 hdc = 1 inch

Instructions

SLIPPERS
Make 2.
For ankle opening, ch 15, join with sl st in first ch to form ring.

Row 1 (RS): For instep, ch 6, sc in 2nd ch from hook, in next 4 chs and in 15 chs around ankle opening, working on opposite side of beg ch on instep, sc in last 5 chs, turn.

Row 2: Ch 2, hdc in each st across, turn.

Row 3: Ch 1, sc in each st across, turn.

Rows 4 & 5: Rep rows 2 and 3.

Row 6: Rep row 2.

Row 7 (WS facing): For sole, fold piece in half lengthwise, working through both thicknesses, ch 1, sl st in next 12 sts. Fasten off.

TOE
*Note: For **dec**, [yo, pull up lp in next st] twice, yo and draw through all 3 lps on hook.*

Rnd 1: Working in ends of rows, join with sc in end of any row, sc in end of each row around opening. *(14 sts)*

Rnd 2: *Dec *(see Note)* in next 2 sts, rep from * around, fasten off leaving an 8-inch length of yarn. Weave yarn around sts and pull to close. Turn slipper RS out.

ANKLE CUFF
Row 1: With RS facing, working on opposite side of beg ch around ankle opening, join with sc in first ch, sc in each st across, turn. *(15 sc)*

Row 2: Ch 2, hdc in each st across, turn.

Row 3: Ch 1, sc in each st across.

Fasten off and weave in all ends.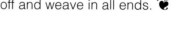

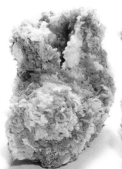

Happy Touch Ripples Baby Afghan

DESIGN BY NANCY NEHRING

SKILL LEVEL ■□□□
BEGINNER

SIZE
38 x 41 inches

MATERIALS
 Patons Astra light (light worsted) weight yarn: 17½ oz/1330 yds/490g #02943 maize yellow *(A)*

 Paton's LuLu medium (worsted) weight yarn: 5¼ oz/402 yds/147g each #36615 yoyo yellow *(B)*, #36128 bunny blue *(C)* and #36717 lemon lime *(D)*

Size H/8/5mm crochet hook or size needed to obtain gauge

GAUGE
15 dc = 4 inches

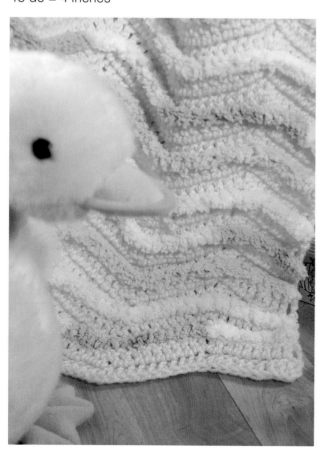

SPECIAL STITCH
Double crochet cluster (dc cl): Yo, insert hook in next st, pull up lp, yo, draw through 2 lps on hook, yo, sk next st, insert hook in next st, pull up lp, yo, draw through 2 lps on hook, yo, draw through all lps on hook.

Instructions

AFGHAN
With A, ch 163.

Row 1 (RS): Working in **back lps** *(see Stitch Guide)* only, dc in 5th ch from hook and in next 7 chs, [dc, ch 1, dc] in next st, *dc in next 8 chs, **dc cl** *(see Special Stitch)* in next st, [dc, ch 1, dc] in next st, rep from * to last 9 chs, dc in next 8 chs, sk next ch, dc in next ch, turn.

Row 2: Ch 3, working in back lps only, sk first st, *dc in next 8 sts, [dc, ch 1, dc] in next st, dc in next 8 sts, dc cl, rep from * to last 9 sts, dc in next 8 sts, sk next st, dc in next st, turn.

Rows 3–64: Rep row 2.

Fasten off and weave in all ends.

HIGHLIGHTED ROWS
Hold Afghan with RS facing, attach D to first front lp between rows 2 and 3, loosely sc in each front lp across. Fasten off.

Rep for each row of front lps on RS, alternating colors C, B, D in sequence. ❧

Little Duckie Baby Booties

DESIGN BY SUE PENROD

SKILL LEVEL EASY

FINISHED SIZE
6 inches long

MATERIALS
 Red Heart Super Saver medium (worsted) weight yarn:
  8 oz/452 yds/226g each #322 pale yellow *(A)* and #354 vibrant orange *(B)*
 Lion Brand Polarspun bulky (chunky) weight yarn:
  1½ oz/137 yds/50g #157 polar yellow *(C)*
Size H/8/5mm double-ended crochet hook or size needed to obtain gauge
Tapestry needle
4 black buttons, ¾-inch-diameter

GAUGE
4 sts = 1 inch; 7 pattern rows = 1 inch

SPECIAL STITCH
Knit stitch (K): Insert hook between front and back bars of indicated vertical st, yo and draw through keeping a lp on hook.

Instructions

BOOTIE
BILL
Row 1: With B, ch 21, working through **back lps** *(see Stitch Guide)* only, insert hook in 2nd ch from hook, yo and draw through forming lp on hook,

*insert hook in next ch, yo and draw through, rep from * across leaving all lps on hook. Slide all lps to opposite end of hook and turn work. Do not cut B. *(21 lps on hook)*

Row 2: To work lps off hook, place A on hook with slip knot, working from left to right draw slip knot through first lp, *yo, draw through 2 lps *(1 lp of each color),* rep from * until 1 lp rem on hook. Do not turn work.

Row 3: Continuing with A and working right to left, sk first vertical bar, **K** *(see Special Stitch)* in each vertical st across. Slide all sts to opposite end of hook, turn.

Rows 4 & 5: With B, rep rows 2 and 3.

Rows 6–17: Rep rows 2–5. Do not fasten off.

SLIPPER BODY
Row 1: With A rep row 2, ch 14, draw up lp in each ch and vertical bar across, ch 14, fasten off. Using A, draw up lp in each ch. *(49 lps on hook)*

Row 2: To work lps off hook, place C on hook with slip knot, working from left to right draw slip knot through first lp, *yo, draw through 2 lps (1 lp of each color), rep from * until 1 lp rem on hook. Do not turn work.

Row 3: Continuing with C and working right to left, sk first vertical bar, K in each vertical st across. Slide all sts to opposite end of hook, turn.

Rows 4 & 5: With A, rep rows 2 and 3.

Rows 6–31: Rep rows 2–5.

Row 32: Sl st in each st across.

FINISHING
With B, sew row ends tog to join. Flatten, sew chain row tog. With C, sew row 1 and row 32 of Bootie body tog to join, forming a tube. Fold tube to inside of Bootie, tacking end rows inside Bootie in place. Sew on button eyes. ❧

Abbreviations & Symbols

beg..beg/beginning
bpdc..back post double crochet
bpsc...back post single crochet
bptr ....back post treble crochet
CC ....contrasting color
ch... chain stitch
ch-...................................refers to chain or space previously
made (i.e. ch-1 space)
ch sp .... chain space
cl(s)...cluster(s)
cm .... centimeter(s)
dc ....double crochet
dec............................... decrease/decreases/decreasing
dtr .... double treble crochet
fpdc.......................................front post double crochet
fpsc...front post treble crochet
fptr ....front post treble crochet
g... gram(s)
hdc ....half double crochet
inc..................................... increase/increases/increasing
lp(s)... loop(s)
MC ....main color
mm... millimeter(s)
oz... ounce(s)
pc .... popcorn
rem ....remain/remaining
rep .... repeat(s)
rnd(s) .... round(s)
RS...right side
sc ....single crochet
sk ....skip(ped)

sl st ....slip stitch
sp(s)...space(s)
st(s)...stitch(es)
tog... together
tr ....treble crochet
trtr ....triple treble crochet
WS .... wrong side
yd(s).. yard(s)
yo...yarn over

* An asterisk is used to mark the beginning of a portion of instructions to be worked more than once; thus, "rep from * twice" means after working the instructions once, repeat the instructions following the asterisk twice more (3 times in all).

[ ] Brackets are used to enclose instructions that are to be worked the number of times indicated after the brackets. For example, "[2 dc in next st, sk next st] 5 times" means to follow the instructions within the brackets a total of 5 times.

( ) Parentheses are used to enclose a group of stitches that are worked in one space or stitch. For example, "(2 dc, ch 2, 2 dc) in next st" means to work all the stitches within the parentheses in the next space or stitch. Parentheses are also used to enclose special instructions or stitch counts.

Skill Levels

BEGINNER

Beginner projects for first-time crocheters using basic stitches. Minimal shaping.

EASY

Easy projects using basic stitches, repetitive stitch patterns, simple color changes and simple shaping and finishing.

INTERMEDIATE

Intermediate projects with a variety of stitches, mid-level shaping and finishing.

EXPERIENCED

Experienced projects using advanced techniques and stitches, detailed shaping and refined finishing.

LEARNING TO ROLL STITCH

The roll stitch is also known as the bullion stitch. Using the yarn and hook specified in the pattern, we suggest that you practice this stitch before using it in your project.

To practice, ch 32. Work 4 sc rows; at the end of the 4th row, ch 3 *(counts as a dc on following rows)*, turn. Then work the next row as follows:

PATTERN ROW 1:

In next sc work roll st as follows:
Step 1: Yo 10 times.
Hint: *Wrap yarn loosely around hook, keeping wraps even.*

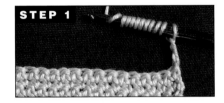

Step 2: Insert hook in st indicated and draw up lp; you now have 12 lps on hook.

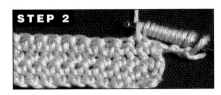

Step 3: Yo and draw through all lps on hook; ch 1.
Hint: *Bring your index finger and thumb (of the hand not holding the hook) up and gently hold the lps on the*

hook *(pinching them just a touch). This makes it easier to pull the hook through all the lps at 1 time. Gently roll the hook around as you pull through.*
Now continue working across row as follows: dc in next sc, [roll st in next sc, dc in next sc] 14 times. Ch 1, turn.

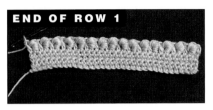

PATTERN ROW 2:

Sc in each dc and each roll st. Ch 3, turn.
Rep Pattern Rows 1 and 2 until you are comfortable with the roll st.
The height of the roll st can vary depending on the number of "yarn overs" that are done.
When you are comfortable with 10 times, try yo 12 times and then 15 and so on.

Standard Yarn Weight System

Categories of yarn, gauge ranges, and recommended needle and hook sizes

Yarn Weight Symbol & Category Names	**1** SUPER FINE	**2** FINE	**3** LIGHT	**4** MEDIUM	**5** BULKY	**6** SUPER BULKY
Type of Yarns in Category	Sock, Fingering, Baby	Sport, Baby	DK, Light Worsted	Worsted, Afghan, Aran	Chunky, Craft, Rug	Super Chunky, Roving
Crochet Gauge* Ranges in Single Crochet to 4 inch	21–32 sts	16–20 sts	12–17 sts	11–14 sts	8–11 sts	5–9 sts
Recommended Hook in Metric Size Range	2.25–3.5 mm	3.5–4.5 mm	4.5–5.5 mm	5.5–6.5 mm	6.5–9 mm	9 mm and larger
Recommended Hook U.S. Size Range	B-1–E-4	E-4–7	7–I-9	I-9–K-10½	K-10½–M-13	M-13 and larger

* GUIDELINES ONLY: The above reflect the most commonly used gauges and hook sizes for specific yarn categories.

HAIRPIN LACE BASIC BRAID

Basic braid is formed by first wrapping yarn around a frame to form a loop. This is accomplished by turning the frame. Then the loop is locked it into place with one single crochet stitch worked into the front of previous loop. These stitches form the rib of the braid. The width of the braid and the size of the loops are determined by the width of the frame you choose or as indicated in the pattern (see photo). The size of the rib is determined by the yarn size, hook size, and stitch used.

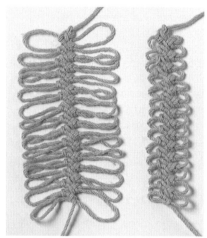

Basic braids with loops of different sizes.

BASIC BRAID INSTRUCTIONS

Step 1: Position frame with spacer at bottom and rods 2½ inches apart. With yarn, make 1¼ inch loop with slip knot and place loop on left rod, having yarn end from skein in front of right rod. Bring yarn around right rod and across back of frame (1).

Step 2: Insert hook through loop from bottom to top (2).

Step 3: Hook yarn and draw through loop (3); ch 1 (4).

Step 4: Drop loop from hook, with hook behind frame. Insert hook from back to front through loop just dropped, turn frame clockwise from right to left keeping yarn to back of frame (loop forms around rod); insert hook under front strand of left loop (5); yo, pull through; yo and pull through 2 loops on hook (6)—single crochet made.

Repeat Step 4 for desired length of braid (7). Finish off by cutting yarn and pull end through last loop on hook.

Hint: *Try to keep the first few single crochet stitches of the rib centered between the rods. After you complete several loops, the single crochet stitches will keep themselves centered.*

Many projects require hairpin strips with more loops than can fit on the frame. When the frame becomes full, count the loops on one rod and mark each 10th, 25th or 50th loop with a marker, such as split ring stitch markers or lengths of yarn. Slide the bottom spacer off of the frame and remove most of the loops. (***Hint:*** *Add ribbon, thread, or yarn to the bottom of each rod and slip loops onto them to keep loops in order.*) Put the spacer back in place and continue making loops.

When additional yarn is needed, add the new yarn along the outside edge of a rod by tying the 2 strands of the old and new yarns together. After strips have been assembled, simply weave the ends through the crochet stitches used to join the strips. On some patterns, you may need to add yarn while crocheting the rib section in order to hide the ends.

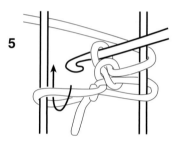
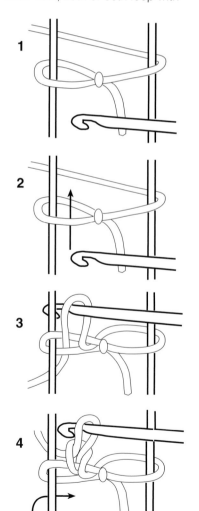
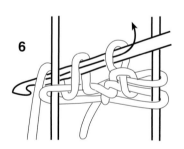
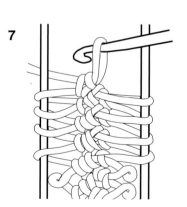

Stitch Guide

CROCHET HOOKS			
Metric	**US**	**Metric**	**US**
.60mm	14	3.00mm	D/3
.75mm	12	3.50mm	E/4
1.00mm	10	4.00mm	F/5
1.50mm	6	4.50mm	G/6
1.75mm	5	5.00mm	H/8
2.00mm	B/1	5.50mm	I/9
2.50mm	C/2	6.00mm	J/10

Chain—ch: Yo, pull through lp on hook.

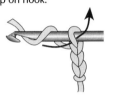

Slip stitch—sl st: Insert hook in st, yo, pull through both lps on hook.

Front loop—front lp Back loop—back lp

Front Loop   Back Loop

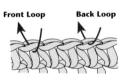

Single crochet—sc: Insert hook in st, yo, pull through st, yo, pull through both lps on hook.

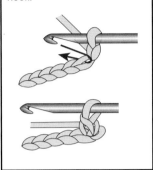

Reverse single crochet— reverse sc: Working from left to right, insert hook in next st, complete as sc.

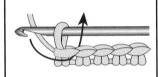

Front post stitch—fp: Back post stitch—bp: When working post st, insert hook from right to left around post st on previous row.

Back   Front

Post of Stitch

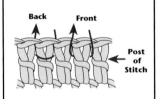

Half double crochet—hdc: Yo, insert hook in st, yo, pull through st, yo, pull through all 3 lps on hook.

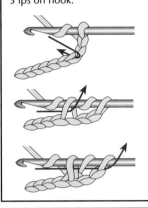

Double crochet—dc: Yo, insert hook in st, yo, pull through st, [yo, pull through 2 lps] twice.

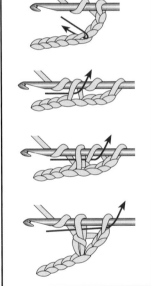

Change colors: Drop first color; with second color, pull through last 2 lps of st.

Treble crochet—tr: Yo twice, insert hook in st, yo, pull through st, [yo, pull through 2 lps] 3 times.

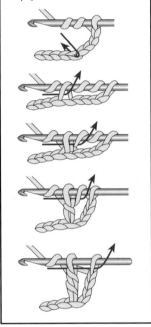

Double treble crochet— dtr: Yo 3 times, insert hook in st, yo, pull through st, [yo, pull through 2 lps] 4 times.

Single crochet decrease (sc dec): (Insert hook, yo, draw up a lp) in each of the sts indicated, yo, draw through all lps on hook.

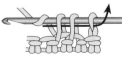

Example of 2-sc dec

Half double crochet decrease (hdc dec): (Yo, insert hook, yo, draw lp through) in each of the sts indicated, yo, draw through all lps on hook.

Example of 2-hdc dec

Double crochet decrease (dc dec): (Yo, insert hook, yo, draw lp through, yo, draw through 2 lps on hook) in each of the sts indicated, yo, draw through all lps on hook.

Example of 2-dc dec

US		UK
sl st (slip stitch)	=	sc (single crochet)
sc (single crochet)	=	dc (double crochet)
hdc (half double crochet)	=	htr (half treble crochet)
dc (double crochet)	=	tr (treble crochet)
tr (treble crochet)	=	dtr (double treble crochet)
dtr (double treble crochet)	=	ttr (triple treble crochet)
skip	=	miss

Special Thanks

We would like to thank the talented crochet designers whose work is featured in this collection.

Cindy Adams
Warm Your Shoulders Soft
    Shrug, 61
Warm-Up With Ripples Afghan, 126
Hot! Hot! Hot! Fiesta Throw, 133
Warming Trend Versatile
    Afghan, 140
Mint Cozy Grannies Baby
    Afghan, 162
So-Soft High-Five Baby Afghan, 165

Edie Eckman
Cuddly & Classy Mom &
    Daughter Sweaters, 77
Festive-Style Cropped
    Cover-Ups, 84
My Blue Denim Wrap Afghan, 134

Darla Fanton
Watercolor Impressions Set, 22

Nazanin Fard
Marvelous Möbius Scarf, 26
From-Elegant-to-Casual Cozy
    Capelet, 53
Scrumptious-to-the-Touch
    Vest, 97

Laura Gebhardt
Foxy Lady Shoulder Wrap, 46
Furry Fun Kid's Poncho, 48
Paris Stitch Captivating Capelet, 50

Ellen Gormley
The Heat's on Hexagon
    Afghan, 128

Tammy Hildebrand
Comfort in the Furry Hood, 28
Fast & Fashionable Soft
    Poncho, 54
Spirited Fur-Trimmed Sweater
    Jacket, 108

Maria Merlino
Make It Furry Hat & Muff, 8
Quick Chullo Hat, 14

Nancy Nehring
Quick & Easy Nouveau Shrug, 113
Happy Touch Ripples Baby
    Afghan, 168

Lisa Pflug
Spirals to Surround You
    Afghan, 122

Bonnie Pierce
Grannies on the Roll Ponchette, 58
Lush & Luxurious Log Cabin
    Afghan, 118
Cozy & Cuddly Mitered Afghan, 136

Sue Penrod
Little Duckie Baby Booties, 170

Joy Prescott
Babette Hat & Scarf, 30
Keep-the-Chill-Out
    Leg Warmers, 33
Little Miss Hat, 156

Janet Rehfeldt
Shoulder-Snuggling Fur Wrap, 56

Diane Simpson
Little Princess Baby Sweater, 152

Darla Sims
Comfy Sweater With Shimmer, 66
Striped-for-Style Fashion Shrug, 69
Pure Huggability Pullover
    Sweater, 72
Green With Envy Sweater
    Jacket, 100
Cool Weather Posh Jacket, 104
Ring-Around-Rosie Afghan &
    Ponchette, 144
Soft-as-Snow Toddler Jacket, 158

Jacqueline Stetter
Just Peachy Set, 17
Get Together for Popcorn
    Ponchos, 39
Layer of Luxury Comfort
    Afghan, 130

Kathleen Stuart
Fuzzy Baby Slippers, 166

Zelda Workman
Fun Hairpin Lace Set, 11
Wardrobe Warming Scarf, 20
Wrap-Yourself-Up Lush Shawl, 42
Soft & Stylish Go-Anywhere
    Ponchette, 44
Soft & Sophisticated Short
    Bolero, 94
Modern-Day Warmth Sofa
    Afghan, 120
Watercolors Baby Set, 146